Multinational Firms and Asian Exports

A Publication of the Economic Growth Center, Yale University

MULTINATIONAL FIRMS
AND ASIAN EXPORTS

BENJAMIN I. COHEN

New Haven and London, Yale University Press, 1975

To Eva

Contents

Diagrams and Tables

Foreword

This volume is one in a series of studies supported by the Economic Growth Center, an activity of the Yale Department of Economics since 1961. The Center is a research organization with worldwide activities and interests. Its research interests are defined in terms of both method of approach and subject matter. In terms of method, the Center sponsors studies which are designed to test significant general hypotheses concerning the problem of economic growth and which draw on quantitative information from national economic accounts and other sources. In terms of subject matter, the Center's research interests include theoretical analysis of economic structure and growth, quantitative analysis of a national economy as an integral whole, comparative cross-sectional studies using data from a number of countries, and efforts to improve the techniques of national economic measurement. The research program includes field investigation of recent economic growth in twenty-five developing countries of Asia, Africa, and Latin America.

The Center administers, jointly with the Department of Economics, the Yale training program in International and Foreign Economic Administration. It presents a regular series of seminar and workshop meetings and includes among its publications both book-length studies and journal reprints by staff members, the latter circulated as Center Papers.

Gustav Ranis, Director

Preface

With hindsight it seems that this book evolved over the last seven years. While working in Washington as an economist for the Agency for International Development (AID), I frequently noticed the statistics on the rapid growth of exports of manufactures from developing countries. At the time I considered such growth to be clearly beneficial to the developing nations.

Upon coming to the Economic Growth Center in 1968, I encountered much discussion of income distribution and the impact of the multinational firm. These were not topics that were widely discussed either in Washington in the mid-1960s or, judging from my dusty lecture notes and reading assignments, in graduate economics courses at Harvard around 1960. Both the tone and the content of the debate at Yale stimulated me to investigate the multinational firm.

Chapter 1 is a general introduction concerning the impact on developing countries of exports by multinational firms. Chapter 2 is a critique of current economic theories about foreign investment and will probably be of interest only to professional economists. Chapter 3 presents the results of my survey of foreign and local firms in Singapore, South Korea, and Taiwan. Because I promised them anonymity, I cannot name the businessmen in these three countries who so generously cooperated with my study. So that they, and others besides professional economists, can read this book, I have put all the mathematical and formal statistical analyses in supplements to chapters 2 and 3 and in appendix A. Those willing to accept the verbal discussion need not look at these parts. The final chapter looks briefly at the noneconomic benefits of foreign investment and discusses what tax policy the developing countries should adopt toward foreign firms.

I will make explicit here that the primary concern of this study is economics, even though the political and social consequences of foreign investment may well dominate the economic ones. I leave these areas to others out of a feeling of relative incompetence, not a lack of interest.

During this investigation I was aided, both intellectually and financially, by others. My first opportunity to study the multinational firm was in South Korea in 1971 under an AID contract with Princeton University. In South Korea I was fortunate to receive the cooperation of O. Wonchol, Assistant Minister for Mining and Industry; Dr. Young Hoon Paik, Director of the Korea Industrial Development Research Institute; Kwang J. Kim of the Institute; Sunki Lee, Director of the Office of Investment Promotion of the Economic Planning Board; Steven Hess of the Board; and Hadley Smith of AID. My trips to Singapore in 1972 and to Taiwan in 1973 were financed under NSF Grant GS33741X. This grant also gave me general financial support during the two years I worked on this study. In Singapore I benefited from the hospitality of the Economic Research Centre of the University of Singapore; Chia Siow Yue assisted in the collection of the data. In Taiwan I received the cooperation of T. K. Tsui, Deputy Secretary-General of the Council for International Economic Cooperation and Development; S. H. Ho of the Council; and James Perng of the Ministry of Economic Affairs.

An AID grant to the Program in Law and Modernization at the Yale Law School enabled me to teach for two years a course on the multinational firm in developing countries. A dialogue with Robert Hudec, who taught with me the first year, and with the students from law and economics who took the course, taught me a great deal.

Over several years I have discussed this research with Carlos Diaz-Alejandro, who also read the entire manuscript (some parts more than once) and made many gentle but helpful comments. Gerald K. Helleiner and Gustav Ranis also read the entire manuscript and offered many useful suggestions. I had long and fruitful discussions on various parts of this study with Thomas Birnberg, Richard Brecher, Richard Nelson, and Vahid Nowshirvani. I was not always wise enough to accept their advice, but even the portion I did accept had a significant effect.

I have been fortunate to have extremely capable research assistants and secretaries. Elizabeth Burgess did most of the data collection and analysis for supplement 2.2. Ann Morgan helped with the computer programming for supplement 2.1. Peter Busch was extremely diligent and capable over a three-year period; his aid extends to all parts of this book. Cheryl Hunt, assisted by Judith Oder and Lorraine Aragon, skillfully typed apparently endless drafts.

My wife and sons cheerfully tolerated my four foreign trips to collect data and my irregular hours in New Haven during the writing of this book. In this, as in my other academic endeavors, their support increased my productivity.

Gratefully acknowledging all this assistance, my final act is to accept complete responsibility for any remaining errors and controversial judgments.

B. I. C.

New Haven, Connecticut
January 1974

1

Introduction

Acting is a business—no more than that—a craft like plumbing, or being an economist; it's been a good living.
                                                                Marlon Brando

EXPORTS AND ECONOMIC DEVELOPMENT

Much of the economic analysis of developing countries involves the search for a crucial factor that distinguishes them from rich countries. Part of this search lies in the definition of developing countries, and part is in the explanation of their existence. In the 1950s economists tended to define developing countries as those with both low per capita incomes and stagnant economies. In the 1960s real gross national product (GNP) grew as fast in the average developing country as in the average rich country,[1] and so the emphasis turned to the low growth of per capita income. In the late 1960s, when countries such as Brazil, Iran, Taiwan, and South Korea achieved an annual rate of growth of per capita income in excess of 5 percent,[2] the definition of the problem of development—at least for these countries—tended to shift to income distribution.

Spurred by the British industrial revolution, economists in the eighteenth and nineteenth centuries assigned a key role to foreign trade in explaining both the growth of national income and its distribution. Recall Adam Smith's discussion of the importance of

1. Between 1960 and 1971 real GNP grew at an annual rate of 5.6 percent in developing countries and 4.7 percent in developed countries. U.S. Agency for International Development, *Gross National Product* (Washington, D.C.: AID, 1972), p. 1.
2. Per capita income in the developed countries rose by 3.3 percent annually from 1965 through 1971. Ibid.

1

an expanding market and David Ricardo's formalization of the
theory of comparative advantage and his analysis of the impact
of the Corn Laws on landlords' incomes. The essence of this early
work still influences economists looking at developing countries
(though contemporary economic theorists looking at growth in rich
countries tend to ignore foreign trade).[3] A casual perusal of Yale
University's card catalogue showed five books published between
1958 and 1968 dealing with international trade and economic
development.[4]

Academic economists tend to argue that a developing nation
should export those items in which it has a comparative advantage. Given appropriate qualifications on the definition of comparative advantage, few would dispute this argument, though some
might question its operational content. These economists also
argue that the government is less likely than the marketplace to
identify these items and that the government should therefore
adopt policies that are neutral among various commodities and
between exporting and producing for the local market. This advice, which has some operational content, can be, and is, dis-
puted.

Many spokesmen for developing countries argue that special
emphasis should be given to exporting manufactures. This view
partially reflects the vision that a modern country needs industry
and that the small domestic markets of most developing countries
will impose high costs unless industrial products are exported.
This position also reflects pessimism about the prospects for a
rapid expansion of exports of primary products (excluding petroleum) from developing countries. Both these themes were ex-
pressed in 1964 by Raúl Prebisch, the articulate and forceful

3. For an example of ignoring foreign trade, see R. M. Solow, *Growth
Theory: An Exposition* (New York: Oxford University Press, 1970).
    4. Gottfried Haberler, *International Trade and Economic Development*
(Cairo: National Bank of Egypt, 1959); Harry G. Johnson, *International
Trade and Economic Growth* (London: Allen and Unwin, 1958); Paul D.
Zook, ed., *Economic Development and International Trade: A Perspective*
(Dallas: Southern Methodist University Press, 1959); Gerald M. Meier,
International Trade and Development (New York: Harper & Row, 1963);
James D. Therberge, ed., *Economics of Trade and Development* (New
York: Wiley, 1968).

spokesman for the developing countries: "While primary commodity exports are, with a few exceptions, expanding relatively slowly, demand for imports of manufactured goods is tending to grow rapidly, at a pace that increases with the rate of development . . . Industrialization based on import substitution has certainly been of great assistance in raising income in . . . developing countries, but it has done so to a much lesser extent than would have been the case had there been a rational policy judiciously combining import substitution with industrial exports." [5]

Relying on this type of analysis, spokesmen for developing countries demanded at the first United Nations Conference on Trade and Development (and on many subsequent occasions) that the rich countries grant temporary preferential tariff treatment for exports of manufactures from developing countries. According to Prebisch, these temporary preferences "would help the industries of developing countries to overcome the difficulties that they encounter in export markets because of their high initial costs." [6]

The rich countries have not granted substantial tariff preferences to the developing countries; [7] many people who accepted the Prebisch diagnosis of the developing countries' export problem are therefore surprised to see how rapidly developing countries' exports have grown in the last decade. Export earnings of developing countries grew by 6.9 percent per year in the 1960s as compared to 2.0 percent per year in the 1950s (table 1.1). Setting aside the nine major oil exporting countries, the annual rate of growth of export earnings of developing countries rose from .7

5. United Nations, *Towards a New Trade Policy for Development* (New York: United Nations, 1964), pp. 3, 21.

6. Ibid., p. 65.

7. The preference scheme introduced by the European Economic Community in 1971 will not, under its present arrangements, have much impact on developing countries' exports. See Richard N. Cooper, "The European Community's System of Generalized Tariff Preferences: A Critique," *Journal of Development Studies* 8 (1972): 379–94. For a similar conclusion encompassing all countries that have granted tariff preferences for exports of manufactures from developing countries, see Tracy Murray, "How Helpful is the Generalised System of Preferences to Developing Countries?" *Economic Journal* 83 (1973): 449–55.

Table 1.1. Exports of Developing Countries by Region

Developing countries	Annual average ($ million, f.o.b.)			Annual percentage change	
	1951–52	1959–60	1969–70	1950s	1960s
Latin America	8,505	9,828	16,229	1.8	5.1
Oil producers[a]	2,248	3,360	3,717	5.2	1.0
Other	6,257	6,468	12,512	.4	6.8
Africa	3,520	4,490	11,235	3.1	9.6
Oil producers[b]	13	12	2,267	−1.0	68.0
Other	3,507	4,478	8,968	3.1	7.2
Middle East	2,535	4,670	10,540	7.9	8.5
Oil producers[c]	1,429	3,127	7,009	10.3	8.4
Other	1,106	1,543	3,531	4.2	8.6
Asia	8,038	7,552	13,660	−.8	6.1
Oil producers[d]	93	95	90	.3	−.5
Other[e]	7,945	7,457	13,570	−.8	6.2
Total above	22,598	26,540	51,664	2.0	6.9
Oil producers	3,783	6,594	13,083	7.2	7.1
Other	18,815	19,946	38,581	.7	6.8
World[f]	75,458	107,814	263,204	4.6	9.4

[a] Venezuela, Netherlands Antilles, and Trinidad.
[b] Libya.
[c] Iran, Iraq, Kuwait, and Saudi Arabia.
[d] Brunei.
[e] Excludes North Korea and North Vietnam.
[f] Excludes mainland China, USSR, Albania, Bulgaria, Czechoslovakia, East Germany, Hungary, Poland, and Rumania.
Source: Various issues of *International Financial Statistics* (Washington, D.C.: International Monetary Fund).

percent in the 1950s to 6.8 percent in the 1960s. In each of the major geographic areas export earnings of developing countries grew more rapidly in the 1960s.

INDUSTRIAL EXPORTS

While much of this acceleration is due to the more rapid growth of exports of primary products other than petroleum,[8] industrial

8. Despite the acceleration in export earnings of primary products, the share of developing countries in world trade of many agricultural com-

exports have grown very rapidly during this period. Using the General Agreement on Tariffs and Trade (GATT) Secretariat's definition of developing countries[9] and a modification of the GATT definition of manufactured exports,[10] developing countries' exports of manufactures rose by about 15 percent per year, from $3.5 billion in 1963 to $9.8 billion in 1970; by 1970 they accounted for about 30 percent of all nonpetroleum exports of developing countries.[11] This growth is even more surprising when one remembers that foreign trade in textiles and clothing, which in 1970 accounted for about one-third of manufactured exports of developing countries, became subject to various international restrictions during the 1960s.

At first glance this rapid growth of industrial exports might be taken as evidence that many developing countries are rapidly becoming "developed," or at least have an efficient manufacturing sector. One might think that the composition of a nation's exports reflects the composition of its output for domestic use.[12]

One's optimism might be tempered, however, by the recollection that the currently less developed countries have had previous spurts in their exports of various commodities. A large literature exists on why the rapid expansion of their exports of primary products in the nineteenth century did not lead to significant economic development in these nations. The general theme of much

---

modities continued to decline in the 1960s. For a further discussion of trends in trade in primary products, see Benjamin I. Cohen and Daniel G. Sisler, "Exports of Developing Countries in the 1960's," *Review of Economics and Statistics* 53 (1971): 354–61.

9. Developing countries include all of Latin America, all of south and east Asia except Japan, all of Africa except the Union of South Africa, and the Middle East.

10. In terms of the Standard International Trade Classification, manufactures include iron and steel (division 67), chemicals (section 5), engineering products (section 7, excluding group 732; and division 69), motor vehicles (group 732), textiles and clothing (divisions 65 and 84), and miscellaneous (section 6, excluding divisions 65, 67, 68, and 69; section 8, excluding division 84). GATT includes and I exclude nonferrous metals (division 84).

11. Data from GATT, *International Trade 1970* (Geneva: GATT, 1971), p. 23; and GATT, *International Trade 1971* (Geneva: GATT, 1972), p. 15.

12. See, for example, Staffan B. Linder, *An Essay on Trade and Transformation* (New York: John Wiley and Sons, 1961).

of this literature is that, in Kindleberger's words, "until the last few years, direct investment in the less developed countries took on an enclave character, in which foreign factors of production—management, capital, and frequently labor—were combined with limited host-country inputs such as a mineral deposit, tropical climate, or in some countries common labor." [13]

Various writers stress different factors in explaining the development of these enclaves. Myint discusses the lack of a domestic transport system and of a smoothly operating market mechanism.[14] Myrdal says, "That the course of events took this 'colonial' character was not mainly due either to the designs of those who provided the capital and built the economic enclaves, or to the intentional policies of their governments. It was much more the natural outcome of the unhampered working of the contemporary market forces." [15] Hymer and Resnick, on the other hand, stress the deliberate policy of the governments of the colonial powers, "as Europe formulated a single strategic conception for the development of the world economy and planned a new division of labor." [16] All these writers agree that foreign firms played a significant role in the development of these enclaves.[17]

In fairness, it should be noted that, as usual, some economists dissent. Vernon says, "Contrary to the hypotheses associated with such well-known development economists as Hans W. Singer, Raúl Prebisch, and Gunnar Myrdal, enclaves of this sort have rarely remained isolated for many decades." [18]

13. Charles P. Kindleberger, *American Business Abroad* (New Haven: Yale University Press, 1969), p. 146.

14. Hla Myint, "The 'Classical Theory' of International Trade and the Underdeveloped Countries," *Economic Journal* 68 (1958): 317–37, reprinted in *Readings in International Economics,* ed. Richard E. Caves and Harry G. Johnson (Homewood, Ill.: Richard D. Irwin, 1968), pp. 318–38.

15. Gunnar Myrdal, *An International Economy: Problems and Prospects* (New York: Harper & Row, 1956), p. 100.

16. Stephen Hymer and Stephen Resnick, "International Trade and Uneven Development," in *Trade, Balance of Payments, and Growth,* ed. Jagdish Bhagwati et al. (Amsterdam: North-Holland Publishing Co., 1971), p. 483.

17. As the cases of Argentina, Australia, and Canada show, an export boom under the auspices of Europeans can facilitate economic development. In none of these three countries was there a large non-European population.

18. Raymond Vernon, *Sovereignty at Bay: The Multinational Spread of U.S. Enterprises* (New York: Basic Books, 1971), p. 49.

Regardless of whether these enclaves lasted for only a few decades or for a longer period, the experience of the last century suggests that one might want to examine the contemporary spurt in manufactured exports in terms of its impact on the developing countries. Is it possible to have an enclave of manufactured exports? Does it matter whether foreign firms account for a large portion of these exports?

MULTINATIONAL FIRMS AND INDUSTRIAL EXPORTS

The reader may wonder whether there is evidence that multinational firms play a large role in the exports of manufactures from developing countries, especially as developing countries frequently complain that multinational manufacturing firms usually prohibit exports by their foreign subsidiaries. For example, 43 percent of all written collaboration agreements between Indian firms and foreign firms from 1961 to 1964 contained clauses restricting exports.[19]

The quantitative data on exports by multinational firms are skimpy, partly because statisticians in government agencies have not been asked to collect and publish such data. For example, the 1966 U.S. Census of U.S. direct foreign investment, which includes data on trade flows, was not published until 1972. As another example, in at least one developing country one government agency has a list of all foreign investments in the country; another government agency has the annual exports of every firm in the country; and nobody has combined these two lists to determine exports by foreign firms.

Definition of Multinational Firms

Even if national governments were to publish foreign trade data on multinational firms, the lack of an international consensus on the definition of a multinational firm means that the data might be inconsistent. In fact, there is not even a consensus on what to call these firms. I will use foreign firm, international firm, and multinational firm as synonyms throughout this book. Most man-

19. Mark Frankena, "Restrictions on Exports by Foreign Investors: The Case of India," *Journal of World Trade Law* 6 (1972): 576.

ufacturing firms are corporations.[20] The problem is to determine
when a firm incorporated in one country is under the control of
a firm incorporated in another country (or a group of individuals
who are citizens of another country). Foreign investment that
does not involve control is considered, in U.S. parlance, to be
"portfolio investment." [21] The problem is to give operational
content to "control."

I give here a sample of some of the current working definitions
of direct foreign investment. The Code of Liberalization of Capital Movements of the Organization for Economic Cooperation
and Development (OECD) defines, in Annex A, direct investment as investment "by non-residents by means of (1) creation
or extension of a wholly-owned enterprise, subsidiary or branch,
acquisition of full ownership of an existing enterprise; (2) par-
ticipation in a new or existing enterprise; (3) a long-term loan
(five years and longer)." The inclusion of long-term loans as a
way of exercising control over a firm recalls Lenin's refusal to
separate direct investment from portfolio investment; he wrote
of "the merging of bank capital with industrial capital, and the
creation, on the basis of this 'finance capital,' of a 'financial oli-
garchy.' " [22] The United States government, in administering its
balance of payments regulations on foreign investment, defines a
direct investor "as any U.S. person having a 10 percent or more
equity or profits interest in a foreign business venture." [23] Decision 24, Article I, of the Commission of the Andean Common
Market (composed of Bolivia, Colombia, Chile, Ecuador, Peru,
and Venezuela) defines a foreign enterprise as one incorporated

20. Because of U.S. tax laws concerning depletion allowances, foreign
investment in extractive industries usually involves the establishment of
foreign branches.
21. As Caves and Jones put it in a recent textbook, "Direct investment
by one country in the economy of another gives its citizens control over the
economic activity in which they invest; portfolio investment does not."
Richard E. Caves and Ronald W. Jones, *World Trade and Payments: An
Introduction* (Boston: Little, Brown and Company, 1973), p. 474.
22. V. I. Lenin, *Imperialism: The Highest Stage of Capitalism* (New
York: International Publishers, 1970), p. 89.
23. "Regulation of Foreign Direct Investment," *United States International Economic Policy in an Interdependent World: Papers Submitted to
the Commission on International Trade and Investment Policy* (Washington, D.C.: U.S. Government Printing Office, 1971), 1:115.

in the recipient country and having less than 51 percent of its capital owned by national investors; other enterprises are either mixed (if nationals own between 51 percent and 80 percent) or national (if nationals own at least 80 percent). The Canadian government, in its 1972 policy statement regulating foreign take-overs of Canadian businesses, said that the acquisition of more than 5 percent of the voting shares of a corporation whose shares are publicly traded will be presumed to bring about control of the corporation.[24]

A U.S. corporation acquiring, say, 7 percent of the voting shares of a Canadian corporation would be considered by the Canadian government to be exercising control over the Canadian corporation but would not be considered by the U.S. government to have made a direct investment. On the other hand, a U.S. corporation owning 15 percent of the equity of a Peruvian corporation would be considered by the U.S. government to have control, but the Andean Commission would consider the Peruvian firm to be a national firm.

Some governments apparently define a foreign firm in terms of the citizenship of its board of directors and chief officers rather than in terms of proportion of equity. Anecdotal evidence suggests this approach is important in textiles, where the government of a developing country allocates its export quotas—which it receives under an international textile agreement—only to local firms; many of these local firms have the vast majority of their capital supplied by foreign textile firms and so would be considered to be foreign firms by foreign governments. For example, by early 1971 Japanese textile firms had made 118 investments in Taiwan, Thailand, Hong Kong, and South Korea, partly in response to U.S. restrictions on textile imports from Japan.[25]

Importance of Multinational Firms

With these ambiguities in mind, I present some scattered bits of evidence on the importance of foreign firms in the export of

24. *New York Times,* 3 May 1972, p. 74.
25. Some of these investments, especially in Thailand, are to serve the local market and are not for export to other countries. "Textiles," *Oriental Economist* 40 (December 1972): 34. I owe this reference to David Mac-Gillis.

manufactures from developing countries. Between 1965 and 1968 annual exports from developing countries by foreign affiliates of U.S. manufacturing firms rose from $700 million to $1,400 million.[26] Between 1957 and 1966 Latin America's annual exports of manufactures rose from $709 million to $1,613 million, and subsidiaries of U.S. firms accounted for 65 percent of this increase of $804 million.[27] In chapter 3 I estimate that in 1971 foreign firms accounted for at least 15 percent of South Korea's $875 million of exports of manufactures, at least 20 percent of Taiwan's $1,428 million of exports of manufactures, and over 50 percent of Singapore's $221 million of exports of manufactures. IBM is said to have been the largest single exporter of manufactures from both Argentina and Brazil in 1969.[28] Foreign firms accounted for at least 35 percent of Colombia's 1970 exports of manufactures and at least 30 percent of Argentina's 1969 exports of manufactures.[29] In 1969 foreign firms accounted for fully 58 percent of $325 million of trade in manufactures within the Latin American Free Trade Association.[30] Firms with foreign technical collaboration agreements accounted for the majority of India's exports of engineering goods in 1968–69.[31] These data support Helleiner's recent conclusion that "the multinational manufacturing firm is likely to play a major role in the future development of manufactured exports from the less-developed countries." [32]

26. *Survey of Current Business,* October 1970, p. 20.
27. *The Effects of United States and Other Foreign Investment in Latin America* (New York: The Council for Latin America, 1970), p. 29.
28. John Tuthill, testimony before the Subcommittee on Foreign Economic Policy of the Joint Economic Committee, in *A Foreign Economic Policy for the 1970's, Part 3—U.S. Policies Towards Developing Countries* (Washington, D.C.: U.S. Government Printing Office, 1970), p. 729.
29. Carlos F. Diaz-Alejandro, "Colombian Imports and Import Controls in 1970/71: Some Quantifiable Features," Yale University, Economic Growth Center Discussion Paper no. 182 (New Haven, July 1973), p. 6; Jorge Katz, "Technology, Dynamic Comparative Advantage and Bargaining Power," mimeographed (Bueno Aires: Instituto Di Tella, n.d.), p. 12.
30. Juan Carlos Casas, "Las Multinacionales y el Comercio Latinoamericano," *Cemla Boletin Mensual* 18 (1972): 606.
31. Mark Frankena, "Restrictions on Exports," p. 589.
32. G. K. Helleiner, "Manufactured Exports from Less-Developed Countries and Multinational Firms," *Economic Journal* 83 (March 1973): 46.

Japan's economic development prior to 1929 may illuminate the impact of multinational firms on economic growth in contemporary developing countries. From 1868 through 1895 there was a negligible inflow of foreign capital into Japan. From 1896 to 1913 there was a substantial inflow of foreign capital, amounting to over two percent of Japan's average national income during the period. From 1914 to 1919 Japan paid off her international debts, and from 1919 to 1929 Japan was a modest international borrower.[33] During the period of heavy capital inflow (1896–1913) direct investment by foreign corporations amounted to only 6 percent of total foreign investment. The remaining 94 percent consisted of foreign loans, almost all of which were to the Japanese government.[34] Most of the foreign investment in Japan by foreign corporations took the form of "joint agreements" with Japanese firms; the foreign firm supplied technical and managerial knowledge.[35]

Is there any evidence that an enclave develops when foreign firms play a large role in the export of manufactures from contemporary developing countries? As chapter 3 will analyze this question in detail for Singapore, South Korea, and Taiwan, I present at this point a summary of recent studies by others of the Mexican "border" industries and of Puerto Rico. In the late 1960s the Mexican government established a zone along the Mexican-U.S. border; firms operating in this zone can import without duty and are exempt from Mexican corporate income tax; they must export their entire output.[36] Almost all the firms are foreign; most of them are owned by U.S. corporations. Border zone exports to the United States rose rapidly, from $7 million

33. Edwin P. Reubens, "Foreign Capital and Domestic Development in Japan," in *Economic Growth: Brazil, India, Japan,* ed. Simon Kuznets, Wilbert Moore, and Joseph Spengler (Durham, N.C.: Duke University Press, 1955), pp. 184–90.
34. Ibid., p. 219.
35. Ibid., pp. 220–21; Saburo Okita and Takeo Miki, "Treatment of Foreign Capital—A Case Study of Japan," in *Capital Movements and Economic Development,* ed. John Adler (New York: St. Martin's Press, 1967), pp. 149–50.
36. For a description of the border industries, see Donald Baerresen, *The Border Industrialization Program of Mexico* (Lexington, Mass.: D. C. Heath and Company, 1971).

in 1966 to $427 million in 1972. The Mexican value added on
these exports is about one-third, almost entirely wages at rates
above the Mexican average. Mexican workers in these industries
spend 50–70 percent of their wages on U.S. commodities.[37] Is this
a contemporary example of the nineteenth-century phenomenon
discussed over twenty years ago by Singer, where "the productive
facilities for export from underdeveloped countries, which were
so largely a result of foreign investment, never became a part of
the internal economic structure of those underdeveloped countries
themselves, except in the purely geographical and physical
sense"? [38]

There may, of course, be consequences for Mexico other than
economic. For example, it is alleged that the development of the
Mexican border industry has led to increases in prostitution, de-
linquency, and illegitimate births; changes in the relationships
between parents and daughters and between husbands and wives;
and deterioration in the quality of housing, sewage, water supply,
and medical care.[39]

Puerto Rico is another possible example of an export enclave.
Since the early 1950s the Puerto Rican government has offered
tax exemption and low-rent land and buildings to mainland U.S.
firms. As Puerto Rico is within the U.S. customs zone, firms import from the mainland without duty and freely export to the
mainland. Richard Weisskoff has analyzed this experience and
found that the rapid growth in industrial output (and exports)
between 1950 and 1970 had little direct impact on the level of
employment despite the rapid growth in per capita GNP.[40]

37. Data for 1966 U.S. imports and for the import component of Mexican wages from U.S. Tariff Commission, *Economic Factors Affecting the
Use of 807.00 and 806.30* (Washington, D.C.: U.S. Government Printing
Office, 1970), pp. 66, 180. I owe this reference to Kenneth Jameson. Data
for 1972 U.S. imports kindly supplied by the U.S. Tariff Commission.

38. H. W. Singer, "The Distribution of Gains Between Investing and
Borrowing Countries," *American Economic Review* 40 (May 1950), re-
printed in *Readings in International Economics*, ed. Richard E. Caves and
Harry G. Johnson (Homewood, Ill.: Richard D. Irwin, 1968), p. 308.

39. These allegations were reported, without comment, by the U.S. Em-
bassy in Mexico, as cited in *Industry Week* 175 (2 October 1972): 34.

40. Richard Weisskoff, "A Multi-Sector Simulation Model of Employment, Growth, and Income Distribution in Puerto Rico: A Re-evaluation

Chapter 2 presents various theories which attempt to deduce the consequences of foreign investment. While this approach has been a powerful technique in the area of foreign trade—indeed some might say too powerful [41]—I conclude that we currently have too many theories about foreign investment and that the theories most consistent with the salient facts of foreign corporate investment do not allow one to conclude that such investment either benefits the host country or increases world output. But these theories do suggest factors which should be examined empirically. Chapter 3 presents the results of my survey of forty-six foreign firms and local firms that are operating in Singapore, South Korea, and Taiwan. My general conclusion, subject to many qualifications, is that the economic benefits of foreign investment are negligible compared with the effects of local firms expanding their exports. The final chapter looks briefly at other benefits of foreign investment and discusses what tax policy the developing countries should adopt toward foreign firms.

---

of 'Successful' Development Strategy," Yale University, Economic Growth Center Discussion Paper no. 174 (New Haven, March 1973).

41. Foreign trade probably has better data, in terms of length of time series and number of countries currently reporting, than any other branch of economics. Yet the ratio of empirical to theoretical work is probably lower for foreign trade than for any other aspect of microeconomics. Have the power and beauty of the theories of Ricardo and Hecksher-Ohlin seduced the best minds? As Kuhn argues, "A paradigm can . . . even insulate the [scientific] community from those socially important problems that are not reducible to the puzzle form, because they cannot be stated in terms of the conceptual and instrumental tools the paradigm supplies." Thomas Kuhn, *The Structure of Scientific Revolutions,* 2nd ed. (University of Chicago Press paperback, 1970), p. 37.

2

Theories of Foreign Investment

The theory that can absorb the greatest number of facts, and persist in doing so, generation after generation, through all changes of opinion and of detail, is the one that must rule all observation.

John Weiss

As a prelude to the empirical findings of the next chapter, I discuss in this chapter some of the major economic theories concerning the impact of foreign investment on the host country. At an early stage of this project, a colleague said to me that the impact is "obviously" beneficial and that the only empirical question is how beneficial. This remark was based, I suspect, on a particular economic theory concerning foreign investment. Other economic theories, less well known to most academic economists, imply that foreign investment may harm the host country. This chapter deals wtih both types of neoclassical theory; I do not consider any Marxian theories. Supplements 2.1 and 2.2 contain the mathematical and econometric bases for the verbal analysis.

After sketching some of the major characteristics of investments by multinational firms, I discuss those theories that assume firms maximize profits in a world where the future is known with perfect certainty, looking first at perfect competition and then at monopoly. I then turn to those theories that emphasize that a large firm makes decisions in the face of great ignorance about the future behavior of the economy and of its rival firms. There is a tension between a theory's being consistent with the observed facts of foreign corporate investment and its yielding precise measures of the impact of such investment on the host country. The theories most consistent with the observed facts give the result that investment may be either harmful or beneficial; the theory that most clearly indicates that investment is beneficial cannot be reconciled with most of the observed facts. Readers who find this statement to be self-evident or are willing to accept it on faith may turn directly to chapter 3.

SALIENT FACTS

I think most scientists would include the ability to explain known facts and to stimulate the search for new facts as important criteria for evaluating a scientific theory. Take, for example, the theory of international trade. Among the broad facts known by the mid-nineteenth century are: (1) all nations have some foreign trade even though there are great differences in their per capita incomes; (2) nations both export and import and continue to do so for long periods of time; and (3) the composition of a nation's exports and imports changes over time. Both the Ricardian theory and the Heckscher-Ohlin theory of comparative advantage explain these facts. Each theory, by emphasizing different factors, stimulated further empirical work after World War II,[1] which, at this time, is too inconclusive to serve as the basis for rejecting either theory. Either theory allows its supporters to reach the broad conclusion that more international trade and investment raises the world's income.[2]

1. See, for example, Wassily Leontief, "Domestic Production and Foreign Trade: The American Capital Position Re-Examined," *Economia Internazionale* 7 (February 1954): 3–32 and G. D. A. MacDougall, "British and American Exports: A Study Suggested by the Theory of Comparative Costs. Part I," *Economic Journal* 61 (December 1951): 697–724.

2. "By permitting every country freely to exchange the produce of its industry when and where it pleases, the best distribution of the labour of the world will be effected, and the greatest abundance of the necessaries and enjoyments of human life will be secured." David Ricardo, *The Principle of Political Economy and Taxation* (New York: E. P. Dutton & Co., 1960), p. 227. "From a world point of view, it is fairly obvious that the redistribution of productive factors throughout the world, whereby a different utilization of various natural resources is made possible, means an increase in the volume of production. . . . All countries profit from economic progress elsewhere." Bertil Ohlin, *Interregional and International Trade*, rev. ed. (Cambridge: Harvard University Press, 1967), pp. 223, 219. Ricardo was more skeptical that all nations benefit from economic progress: "Trade with a colony may be so regulated that it shall at the

What are the basic facts that a contemporary theory of direct foreign investment should explain? I suggest the following, with no particular importance attached to the order: (1) most direct foreign investment is done by corporations rather than by individuals; (2) most direct foreign investment is done by a relatively few very large firms; (3) the propensity for U.S. firms to invest abroad differs considerably among industries; (4) within the same industry there is a two-way flow of direct foreign investment; (5) sometimes a nation's corporations control foreign firms while at the same time some of its corporations are controlled by foreign firms; (6) for U.S. manufacturing corporations during the last decade the reported rate of profit on foreign investment was about the same as on U.S. domestic investment; (7) in recent years the majority of U.S. direct investment has been financed by funds raised outside the United States; and (8) the same U.S. companies that are large investors are also large traders. For those readers unfamiliar with the recent literature on direct foreign investment, I will summarize here the evidence in support of each of these eight broad facts.

1 and 2. The 1966 survey of U.S. foreign direct investment counted all persons and firms with foreign direct investment in excess of $50,000. About 3,400 persons and firms—less than one percent of all U.S. corporations—replied; their total foreign assets were $583 billion.[3] About 39 percent of those assets were owned by only 298 U.S. firms,[4] which approximates the concentration of all U.S. corporate assets; in 1964, 325 companies had 42 percent of all assets of U.S. nonfinancial institutions.[5]

Even among large U.S. companies, it is the very largest which do most of the foreign direct investment. Raymond Vernon ex-

same time be less beneficial to the colony, and more beneficial to the mother country, than a perfectly free trade." Ricardo, *Political Economy*, p. 231.

3. U.S. Department of Commerce, *U.S. Direct Investments Abroad 1966, Part 1: Balance of Payments Data* (Washington, D.C.: U.S. Government Printing Office, 1970), p. 28.

4. U.S. Department of Commerce, *Special Survey of U.S. Multinational Companies, 1970* (Washington, D.C.: U.S. Government Printing Office, 1972), p. 3.

5. F. M. Scherer, *Industrial Market Structure and Economic Performance* (Chicago: Rand McNally and Co., 1970), p. 40.

amined all those firms on the *Fortune* 500 list in 1963 and 1964 and found that 187 of these firms, which he called "multinational," controlled 80 percent of the 2,500 manufacturing subsidiaries controlled by the top 500 firms. These 187 firms had average annual sales in 1964 of $927 million, as compared with $283 million for the other firms on the *Fortune* 500 lists and $2 million for the average U.S. manufacturing firm.[6]

3. Vernon sorted these 187 firms into twenty-three industries. These firms dominate some industries; they are a minority in other industries. For example, in 1966 these 187 firms accounted for 85 percent of the total sales of all U.S. firms making motor vehicles and equipment and 77 percent of the total sales of all U.S. drug firms but only 5 percent of the total sales of all firms producing primary iron and steel.[7]

4. When U.S. firms invest in foreign countries, foreign firms in the same industry invest in the United States; Stephen Hymer stressed this phenomenon over a decade ago.[8] The U.S. Department of Commerce lists 378 foreign firms that had at least one manufacturing subsidiary in the United States by 1969.[9] There are more recent cases. In 1972, Sony built a plant in the United States to produce television sets[10] while U.S. firms were building television factories in the Far East.

5. While U.S. direct investment abroad far exceeds foreign direct investment in the United States,[11] there is more balance in some countries. For example: in 1970 about 200 foreign companies had manufacturing subsidiaries in Sweden. These subsidiaries had assets of Kr. 6.9 billion, sales of Kr. 10.1 billion, and

6. Raymond Vernon, *Sovereignty at Bay: The Multinational Spread of U.S. Enterprises* (New York: Basic Books, 1971), pp. 11, 8.

7. Ibid., pp. 14–15.

8. Stephen Hymer, "The International Operations of National Firms: A Study of Direct Foreign Investment" (Ph.D. diss., Massachusetts Institute of Technology, 1960).

9. Sidney Rolfe, ed., *The Multinational Corporation in the World Economy* (New York: Praeger Publishers, 1969), pp. 131–67.

10. *New York Times*, 18 March 1973, sec. 3, p. 1.

11. In 1970 foreign direct investment assets in manufacturing in the United States had a book value of $6.1 billion. U.S. direct investment assets in manufacturing in foreign countries had a book value of $32.2 billion. *Survey of Current Business*, October 1971, pp. 38, 29.

employed 65,000 persons. In the same year Swedish manufacturing companies had foreign subsidiaries with assets of Kr. 15.6 billion, sales of Kr. 16 billion, and a total payroll of 183,000 persons.[12]

6. Reported average profits on foreign investment by U.S. manufacturing firms are about the same as, or perhaps even slightly less than, profits on domestic U.S. investment. While return on foreign manufacturing investment slightly exceeded that on domestic investment in several recent years, during the 1960s the yield on domestic manufacturing investment averaged 12.4 percent, as compared to 11.8 percent on direct foreign manufacturing investments.[13] Those who wish to believe that firms are maximizing profits explain these data in one of three ways: (i) Firms maximize expected long-term profits, and we only observe actual short-term profits. (ii) By manipulating "transfer prices" among subsidiaries in various countries, international firms are able to report their largest profits where the marginal tax rates are lowest; to explain the observed profit data, however, this argument requires that the marginal corporate tax rate be lower in the United States than in the rest of the world. And (iii) international firms are able to avoid complete reporting of some of their foreign profits.[14]

7. Very little foreign investment by U.S. firms is financed by funds from the United States. This was true even before 1968, when the U.S. government imposed mandatory restraints on the outflow of funds from the United States. Plant and equipment expenditures in manufacturing by foreign affiliates of U.S. corporations averaged $4.3 billion per year between 1965 and 1967 and $5.2 billion per year between 1968 and 1970. Net capital outflow from the United States by manufacturing firms averaged $1.5 billion per year from 1965 through 1967 and $1.1 billion

12. Hans-Frederick Samuelsson, *Foreign Direct Investment in Sweden 1965–70* (Stockholm: Industriens Utrednings-Institut, 1973), pp. 6, 9.
13. *Survey of Current Business,* October 1970, pp. 32, 33.
14. For a discussion of possible ways to avoid reporting profits by using differences in national tax treatment of depreciation, see Walter A. Slowinski and Thomas M. Haderlein, "United States Taxation of Foreign Income: The Increasing Role of the Foreign Tax Credit," in *International Trade, Investment, and Organization,* ed. Wayne R. LaFave and Peter Hay (Urbana: University of Illinois Press, 1967), pp. 137–53.

per year from 1968 through 1970.[15] Thus net capital outflow from the United States financed about 35 percent of foreign investment in manufacturing from 1965 through 1967 and about 22 percent from 1968 through 1970. The remainder was financed by the foreign affiliates' retained earnings, depreciation allowances, and foreign borrowing.

8. Of the 298 U.S. companies mentioned earlier, 223 are manufacturing companies. In 1970 those 223 companies had investments in foreign affiliates—net plant and equipment, stocks, and advances—of $91 billion. These 223 companies also accounted in 1970 for $17 billion of U.S. exports and $9 billion of U.S. imports. These firms were therefore involved, in 1970, in 58 percent of total U.S. exports of manufactures and 36 percent of total U.S. imports of manufactures. About 42 percent of the exports and 45 percent of the imports of these 223 U.S. manufacturing companies involved transactions with a majority-owned foreign affiliate.[16]

With these facts as background, let us turn to the various economic theories about foreign direct investment. While developing countries are occasionally the source of foreign investment,[17] they are usually the recipient, and so I shall explore each theory for its predicted consequences for the host country. I shall look at the consequences in terms of both the size of national income and its distribution among various groups.

Profit Maximization and Certainty

Perhaps because of the Ricardian emphasis on the international immobility of capital and labor, economic theory has had rela-

15. Data on plant and equipment expenditures from *Survey of Current Business*, September 1971, p. 28. Data on capital outflow from *Survey of Current Business*, October 1971, p. 29.

16. Manufacturing excludes petroleum. Data on trade of these companies from U.S. *Special Survey*, p. 87. Total U.S. trade in manufactures from *Economic Report of the President 1973* (Washington, D.C.: U.S. Government Printing Office, 1973), p. 295.

17. South Korean firms are now investing in other countries. Producing such things as timber, instant noodles, and fountain pens, twenty-three South Korean companies have invested $13 million in eighteen countries. *New York Times*, 19 March 1973, p. 58.

tively little to say about the impact of international investments by corporations. MacDougall's article is one of the few theoretical analyses in this area. Caves and Johnson, in 1968, wrote that "MacDougall's essay on foreign investment . . . points out the special characteristics of this form of international factor movement." [18] Other readers of MacDougall's article may not easily discern these special characteristics, and at the end of his article MacDougall says that "no distinction is made between fixed interest and equity investment." [19] Supplement 2.1 contains MacDougall's formal analysis and a formal critique. Assuming, among other things, perfect competition, he concludes that "the most important direct gains . . . from more rather than less private investment from abroad seem likely to come through higher tax revenue from foreign profits (at least if the higher investment is not induced by lower tax rates), through economies of scale and through external economies generally, especially where [local] firms acquire 'know-how' or are forced by foreign competition to adopt more efficient methods." [20] However, the host country may be worse off, according to MacDougall, if foreign firms are in such a monopolistic position that they exploit local buyers.[21]

This last qualification in MacDougall's analysis is at the core of less formal analyses by other economists. As Carlos Diaz-Alejandro put it, "Much [direct foreign investment] in Latin America has occurred in areas and sectors where markets and competition are weak. [Pure competitive models] would miss most of what the argument is about." [22]

Even within the framework of perfect competition, MacDougall's analysis has several weaknesses. It pays only slight attention to the impact of better management and the technology brought

18. Richard E. Caves and Harry G. Johnson, eds., *Readings in International Economics* (Homewood, Ill.: Richard D. Irwin, 1968), p. vii.

19. G. D. A. MacDougall, "The Benefits and Costs of Private Investment from Abroad: A Theoretical Approach," *Economic Record* 36 (March 1960), reprinted in Caves and Johnson, *Readings in International Economics*, p. 193.

20. Ibid.

21. Ibid., p. 186.

22. Carlos F. Diaz-Alejandro, "Direct Foreign Investment in Latin America," in *The International Corporation*, ed. Charles P. Kindleberger (Cambridge, Mass.: M.I.T. Press, 1970), p. 319.

by foreign firms.[23] By using a one-sector model, his approach also ignores the consequences of having foreign investment in only one part of the economy. These omissions are important because, as Richard Brecher has pointed out, in a two-sector model foreign capital has no effect on the national income of a small country unless it brings a new technology or changes behavior. This conclusion follows from the "Rybczynski effect:" with world prices fixed, perfect competition, full employment, universal profit maximization, and a given linear homogeneous production function in each sector, the arrival of foreign capital has no impact on the domestic wage or interest rate and hence no impact on national income.[24]

The impact of bringing more capital and a different technology to a developing country may be studied in either a one-sector or a two-sector model. Supplement 2.1 gives a simple mathematical example of a one-sector model where foreign capitalists, behaving as perfect competitors, bring capital and a new technology which reduces the income accruing to all the natives, increases the income accruing to local capitalists, and reduces the income accruing to local workers. A second mathematical example presents a two-sector model where foreign capitalists, behaving as perfect competitors, bring capital and a new technology which so transform the economy that there is a trade-off between increasing national income and raising labor's income.

In MacDougall's model firms move capital among countries in order to increase profits in a world of perfect certainty. This model does not explain why so few firms invest in foreign countries, why the propensity to invest differs among industries, why there is two-way investment in the same industry, why most U.S. foreign investment is financed from foreign sources, or why the same firm both exports and invests in foreign countries.

There are also models, less mathematical, which emphasize the maximization of profits in a monopolistic environment. The

23. MacDougall notes that the introduction of a heavily labor-saving technology could make the host country worse off. MacDougall, "Benefits and Costs," p. 182.

24. T. M. Rybczynski, "Factor Endowment and Relative Commodity Prices," *Economica* 22 (November 1955): 336–41, reprinted in Caves and Johnson, *Readings in International Economics*.

earliest contemporary statement of this point of view was by Stephen Hymer, who says, in Kindleberger's words, "for direct investment to thrive there must be some imperfection in markets for goods or factors, including among the latter technology, or some interference in competition by government or by firms, which separate markets." [25] The emphasis on monopoly will remind some readers of Lenin's contention that "imperialism is the monopoly stage of capitalism." [26] As Hymer put it more recently, "Direct foreign investment . . . is . . . an instrument for restraining competition between firms of different nations." [27] This approach explains why most investors are large firms, why the propensity to invest differs among industries, why there is two-way investment, and why investment does not involve the transfer of much capital. It does not explain why the profit rate on foreign investment is no higher than on domestic investment.

Harry Johnson uses this analysis to concentrate on the foreign firm's monopolization of knowledge: "The transference of knowledge . . . is the crux of the direct investment process." [28] Viewing the firm as a discriminating monopolist maximizing its profits by selling knowledge to various countries, Johnson argues that the developing countries will pay the foreign firm less for the knowledge than will rich countries because "poorer and less-developed countries are likely to have more elastic demand curves for knowledge-intensive products than richer and more advanced countries." [29] My casual observation suggests that developing countries do pay less for movies, but Johnson, unfortunately, gives no evidence for his assertion.

Another problem with Johnson's approach is that he views the purchaser's demand curve for foreign knowledge as equally stable and well defined in both rich and poor countries. For most items

25. Charles P. Kindleberger, *American Business Abroad* (New Haven: Yale University Press paperback, 1969), p. 13.

26. V. I. Lenin, *Imperialism: The Highest Stage of Capitalism* (New York: International Publishers, 1970), p. 88.

27. Stephen Hymer, "The Efficiency (Contradictions) of Multinational Corporations," *American Economic Review* 60 (May 1970): 443.

28. Harry G. Johnson, "The Efficiency and Welfare Implications of the International Corporation," in Kindleberger, ed., *International Corporation*, p. 35.

29. Ibid., p. 41.

the consumer can easily learn about the relative quality of similar products and can compare qualities with prices. For these items a private marketplace gives an "efficient" result. As Arrow noted a decade ago, for some purchases, such as medical care, the private marketplace is less likely to give an "efficient" result because "the value of information is frequently not known in any meaningful sense to the buyer; if, indeed, he knew enough to measure the value of information, he would know the information itself." [30] Similarly, in developing countries there may be few, if any, persons who know enough to evaluate the knowledge being sold by different foreign firms. In my view, the price is more likely to be the result of a bargaining process than to be determined by the neat intersection of a known marginal revenue curve and a known marginal cost curve. The developing country, having nobody who knows, for example, about electronics, may pay a higher price to an international firm that sells electronic communications equipment than a rich country which has many knowledgeable citizens who, if they do not have direct knowledge of the product, will at least know enough to choose a competent consultant from among the many technical consulting firms. [31] If, as argued earlier and in supplement 2.1, the introduction of foreign technology can reduce national income and affect its distribution when foreign firms act as perfect competitors, the consequences of foreign investment will be even more severe if the foreign firm prices its technology in a more monopolistic fashion.

A final problem with Johnson's approach is that he views the foreign firm's monopoly as being in "the application of superior commercial knowledge." [32] Caves, on the other hand, argues that "product differentiation [is] one necessary characteristic of indus-

---

30. Kenneth J. Arrow, "Uncertainty and the Welfare Economics of Medical Care," *American Economic Review* 53 (December 1963): 946.

31. Making a correct choice of foreign technology is a problem even when the foreign technology is not owned by a multinational firm. Evenson concludes that those developing countries that gained most from the "green revolution" in wheat and rice were the ones that had significant indigenous research capability. Robert Evenson, "International Diffusion of Agrarian Technology," *Journal of Economic History* 34 (March 1974): 65.

32. Johnson, *Efficiency and Welfare Implications*, p. 39.

tries in which substantial direct investment occurs." [33] These two
views lead to different implications for the welfare of the host
country. Introducing a broader variety of products may lead to
excess capacity, more advertising, and the creation of new consumer demands.[34] Johnson, following most economists, rejects
the notion that firms can create demand for a new product[35] and
therefore concludes that "the transplantation of superior technical
and managerial knowledge is most probably beneficial to a country
receiving foreign direct investment." [36]

Some of those who analyze foreign investment in terms of monopoly see the problem as being a temporary one. Kindleberger,
for example, says that "in the bilateral monopoly . . . game rep-
resented by direct investment in the less-developed country, there
has been a steady shift in the advantages from the side of the
company to that of the country." [37] His examples refer, however,
to multinational firms exporting natural resources from a developing country. It is less clear that a government can tax the
profits of a foreign company producing manufactures for export.
As *Fortune* put it, "The developing countries' contribution . . .
will be reserves of low-cost and teachable labor." [38] There being
several developing countries which have demonstrated a capacity
to supply this kind of labor, it is difficult for just one of them to
tax the monopoly profits of a foreign firm. The foreign firm will
either move to another developing country or arrange its transfer
prices so as to show little profit in the nation trying to tax monopoly profits.[39] I return to this point in chapter 4.

33. Richard E. Caves, "International Corporations: The Industrial Economics of Foreign Investment," *Economica* 38 (February 1971): 5.
34. For a statement concerning the deleterious effects of creating new
demands, see John Kenneth Galbraith, *The Affluent Society* (Boston:
Houghton Mifflin Co., 1958), esp. chapters 10 and 11.
35. "The demand curve for the new product . . . [is] assumed to be
latent in the utility functions of consumers." Johnson, *Efficiency and Welfare Implications*, p. 37.
36. Ibid., p. 39.
37. Kindleberger, *American Business Abroad*, p. 150.
38. "The Poor Countries Turn from Buy-Less to Sell-More," *Fortune*
81 (April 1970): 91.
39. For other skeptical views of the bargaining strength of developing
countries, see Paul Streeten, "Technology Gaps Between Rich and Poor
Countries," *Scottish Journal of Political Economy* 19 (November 1972):

Uncertainty

Both the competitive model and the monopoly model just discussed assume the firm knows everything about the future. Consider now the implications of the fact that firms, like individuals, operate in an uncertain and unstable world. In large firms, as Keynes put it, "the shareholders are almost entirely dissociated from the management, with the result that the direct personal interest of the latter in the making of great profit becomes quite secondary. When this stage is reached, the general stability and reputation of the institution are more considered by the management than the maximum of profit for the shareholders." [40]

The Tobin-Markowitz theory implies that a low (or negative) correlation between foreign and domestic risks can make foreign investment attractive even if its risk is higher and its rate of return is lower than domestic investment because foreign investment will reduce a firm's total risk. [41] This theory would also explain two-way investment in the same industry, since firms from two countries could each reduce total risks by investing in the other country. Finally, by considering differences among various industries in the correlations among national markets, this theory could also explain differences among various industries in the propensity to invest in foreign countries.

While this theory has recently been applied to long-term inter-

222; and G. K. Helleiner, "Manufacturing for Export: Multinational Firms and Economic Development," *World Development* 1 (July 1973): 13–21.

40. John Maynard Keynes, *Essays in Persuasion* (London: Rupert Hart-Davis, 1952), pp. 314–15.

41. Let x be the variable—such as sales or profits—on which management focuses. Let p be the proportion of x in country 1 and $1 - p$ the proportion in country 2. Let r be the correlation between x in country 1 and x in country 2. Let v_{1+2}^2 be the total variance of x, v_1^2 the variance of x in country 1, and v_2^2 be the variance of x in country 2. Then:

$$v_{1+2}^2 = p^2 v_1^2 + 2p(1 - p)r\, v_1 v_2 + (1 - p)^2 v_2^2.$$

For example, suppose the variance of sales is nine in one country and sixteen in another country and the correlation between sales in the two countries is .25; then having half of a firm's sales in each country gives a variance for the firm's worldwide sales of 7.75. So firms in both countries reduce their variance through foreign investment.

national portfolio investment[42] and to international trade,[43] it has not been applied by economists who study direct corporate investment. Nor do those economists who stress the need for large firms to reduce uncertainty deal with foreign investment. Galbraith, for example, ignores foreign investment as a possible way for the technostructure to reduce uncertainty over earnings and sales, though he deals with product diversification as a way of increasing a corporation's stability.[44] Marris also concentrates on the corporation's development of new products.[45]

On the other hand, the president of a large U.S. firm with plants in thirty-three countries said, "We know . . . that our worldwide operations cushion the impact on the corporation as a whole of a recession in any one country. This has, in effect, given our total operations more stability." [46] A recent survey of thirty-five large U.S. multinational firms revealed that many executives feel that "when a U.S. company has affiliates in many non-U.S. markets, it is less exposed to the vagaries of the business cycle in the U.S. market." [47] Supplement 2.2 contains statistical tests which also

42. Herbert G. Grubel, "Internationally Diversified Portfolios: Welfare Gains and Capital Flows," *American Economic Review* 58 (December 1968): 1299–1314. Norman C. Miller and Marina V. N. Whitman, "A Mean-Variance Analysis of United States Long-Term Portfolio Foreign Investment," *Quarterly Journal of Economics* 84 (May 1970): 175–96; Haim Levy and Marshall Sarnat, "International Diversification of Investment Portfolios," *American Economic Review* 60 (September 1970): 668–75.

43. William C. Brainard and Richard N. Cooper, "Uncertainty and Diversification in International Trade," *Studies in Agricultural Economics, Trade, and Development* 8 (1968): 257–85; and Seev Hirsch and Baruch Lev, "Sales Stabilization Through Export Diversification," *Review of Economics and Statistics* 53 (1971): 270–77.

44. John Kenneth Galbraith, *The New Industrial State* (Boston: Houghton Mifflin Co., 1967), p. 38.

45. Robin Marris, "The Modern Corporation and Economic Theory," in *The Corporate Economy: Growth Competition and Innovative Potential*, ed. Robin Marris and Adrian Wood (Cambridge: Harvard University Press, 1971), pp. 271–83.

46. James M. McKee, Jr., testimony before the Subcommittee on Foreign Economic Policy of the Joint Economic Committee, July 27–30, 1970, in *A Foreign Economic Policy for the 1970's, Part 4—The Multinational Corporation and International Investment* (Washington, D.C.: U.S. Government Printing Office, 1970), p. 767.

47. *The Effects of U.S. Corporate Foreign Investment 1960–1970* (New York: Business International Corporation, 1972), p. 14.

suggest that firms invest in foreign countries in order to reduce their global risks and that the scope for such reduction differs among industries. These tests are done in terms of both sales and profits, since there is no consensus that the managements of large firms are very concerned with corporate profits.

The conclusion that U.S. firms invest overseas in order to reduce their risks would be important for those countries which seek to attract foreign investment. Foreign countries, especially developing countries, advertise incentive schemes designed to increase the foreign firm's profits and also emphasize the stability of the country.[48] Could a country also attract foreign investment by emphasizing the low (or negative) correlation of its fluctuations with those of other countries? Rather than claiming, for example, that workers never strike, a foreign government could claim they never strike in years when workers in other countries are on strike.[49]

A judgment on the motivation for foreign investment is also important because economists frequently deduce the impact of foreign investment from the assumption that firms seek only to maximize profits. As Caves put it, "In the absence of externalities and market imperfections, the case for free movement of direct investment as a means of maximizing world welfare is simply the case for allowing any factor or product to flow towards locations where it has the greatest excess of marginal value over marginal cost." [50] Caves, of course, stresses that much international investment seems to depend on market imperfections even if one assumes firms are maximizing profits. The recent U.S. Presidential Commission seems to ignore this qualification in saying that "the international investment process may be viewed as the movement of productive resources from areas of lesser to areas of greater relative opportunity, thereby improving the world's allocation of

48. The government of Taiwan, for example, notes as evidence of the favorable climate for foreign investment that "there has been no strike on the island in more than two decades." *Foreign-Invested Enterprises in Taiwan, Republic of China* (Taipei: Council for International Economic Cooperation and Development, 1972), p. 8.

49. Some labor unions have realized this problem and are coordinating their international activities. See "Multinational Firms Face a Growing Power: Multinational Unions," *Wall Street Journal,* 23 April 1973, p. 1.

50. Caves, "International Corporations," p. 22.

resources to the mutual benefit of parent, host, and other countries."[51]

Although foreign investment may reduce the global risk of the multinational firm, it may increase the risks faced by a developing country. The multinational firm is subject to pressures in many more countries than is the local firm, and the developing country may be viewed as marginal to the multinational firm exporting to rich countries. Stobaugh, for example, reports that one U.S. electronics firm responded to the 1969–70 decline in U.S. radio sales by stopping production in its new Taiwan plant rather than curtailing production in its U.S. plant.[52]

While each firm may feel it is reducing its own risk through foreign investment, the actions of all the international firms may reduce the stability of some national economies and increase the stability of others, or perhaps even reduce the economic stability of all countries. The impact on a national economy depends on the policies (e.g., change in the exchange rate, direct controls, monetary or fiscal policy) the government adopts in response to instability.

Until now I have considered only the uncertainty stemming from the lack of a perfect correlation among various nations' economies. What about the uncertainty stemming from the reactions of rival firms in the same industries? There is substantial evidence that most direct foreign investment is done by large firms that are in oligopolistic industries.[53] In such industries it is quite

51. *United States International Economic Policy in an Interdependent World: Report to the President Submitted by the Commission on International Trade and Investment Policy* (Washington, D.C.: U.S. Government Printing Office, 1971), p. 173.

52. Robert B. Stobaugh, "How Investment Abroad Creates Jobs at Home," *Harvard Business Review* 50 (September–October 1972): 122–23.

53. See, for example, Vernon, *Sovereignty at Bay*, especially chapters 1 and 3.

The econometric evidence is less clear. Using ninety-five three-digit U.S. manufacturing industries, Wolf found in a cross-section study for 1963 that sales of foreign affiliates relative to U.S. output of the industry were significantly affected by average firm size in the industry, technical manpower as a proportion of industry employment, and the profit rate in the industry. The level of concentration in the industry was not significant. Concentration was significant, however, in a cross-section regression explaining exports plus foreign affiliate sales as a percentage of U.S. output. As Wolf notes, a better test of the importance of concentration would use

possible that most firms will imitate the investment behavior of the firm which first invests abroad.[54] As Aharoni put it, "When several companies in the same industry went abroad, others felt compelled to follow suit in order to maintain their relative size and their relative rate of growth . . . imitating the commitments of a leader on the grounds that one is less vulnerable if his exposures are the same as those of his principal competitors." [55]

One can make more formal the notion that in an uncertain world firms in an oligopolistic industry will follow any firm which invests abroad. Consider an industry with two U.S. firms, each of which sells in the United States and is deciding whether to continue production in the United States or to invest in a less developed country (LDC) for export to the United States. Suppose total industry sales are independent of production costs (at least within the range considered in this example). Each firm faces two kinds of uncertainty: what will its rival do, and how will costs in the LDC compare with those in the United States. The latter uncertainty stems from such factors as the future of the exchange rate for the dollar, future U.S. tariff levels, and future productivity levels and wages in the LDC relative to those in the United States. Each firm is assumed to perceive the same payoff matrix, as shown in table 2.1 with hypothetical numbers: firm A's profits are shown to the left, and firm B's profits to the right. For example, if firm A invests in the LDC and firm B does not and if costs in the LDC turn out to be lower than costs in the United States, then firm A's profits are $20 and firm B has profits of $4. If firm A invests in the LDC and firm B does not and if

---

firm data rather than industry data. Bernard M. Wolf, *Internationalization of U.S. Manufacturing Firms: A Type of Diversification* (Ph.D. diss., Yale University, 1971).

54. Fifteen years ago Duesenberry argued that in an oligopolistic industry "it is important . . . for every firm to cut costs as fast as its rivals do. But that can be achieved equally well whether all the firms follow a cautious policy and reduce costs slowly, or adopt a daring policy and reduce costs rapidly. . . . the firm which is willing to take the greatest risks will set the pace of investment and research expenditures which in the long run set the level of costs." James Duesenberry, *Business Cycles and Economic Growth* (New York: McGraw-Hill Book Co., 1958), pp. 130–31.

55. Yair Aharoni, *The Foreign Investment Decision Process* (Boston: Harvard University Graduate School of Business Administration, 1966), pp. 65–66.

Table 2.1. Hypothetical Profits
(Firm A, firm B)

	LDC is *low cost*	*LDC is* *high cost*
Neither firm invests	10, 10	10, 10
Only firm A invests	20, 4	4, 20
Only firm B invests	4, 20	20, 4
Both firms invest	12, 12	5, 5

production costs in the LDC turn out to be higher than in the United States, then firm A earns $4 and firm B earns $20.[56]

Suppose each firm follows a strategy of maximizing its minimum profit. If firm B thinks firm A will invest in the LDC, then firm B will also invest, since investing implies a profit for firm B of at least $5, as compared to a possible profit of only $4 if it does not invest. If firm B thinks firm A will not invest in the LDC, then firm B will also not invest in the LDC. Therefore, once firm A invests, firm B will also invest even though firm B is still uncertain as to whether production costs will be lower in the LDC than in the United States. Similarly, if firm B invests first in the LDC, firm A will follow suit. I will discuss the taxation implications of this analysis in chapter 4.

CONCLUSION

It follows from the above analysis that the mere act of foreign investment does not allow one to conclude that international firms are moving resources from an area where their productivity is low to an area where it is high. In a world where corporations invest in foreign countries in response to uncertainty about the behavior of national economies and their industry rivals, foreign investment may not increase either the world's output or the income

56. Those who feel management concentrates on sales can consider the matrix as showing sales rather than profits for different strategies. Knickerbocker has measured the extent to which foreign investment by U.S. firms clusters in a relatively short time period and has attempted to explain the variability in this clustering. Frederick T. Knickerbocker, *Oligopolistic Reaction and Multinational Enterprise* (Boston: Harvard University Graduate School of Business Administration, 1973).

of any particular nation. A theory that sees foreign investment as a response to uncertainty is consistent with many of the salient facts about U.S. foreign investment: investment by a few large firms, differences among industries in propensity to invest abroad, two-way investment in the same industry, and the same profit rate on foreign and domestic investments. Such a theory does not, however, lead to any particular deduction about the consequences of foreign investment. Those desiring such deductions must turn to theories in which profits are maximized with complete certainty, either by a monopolist or by competitive firms.

The perfectly competitive model assumes that foreign firms and local firms both operate in the same way (e.g., use the same technology, are equally efficient, and respond to the same market stimuli) and emphasizes the movement of capital from nations where its rate of return is low to nations where it is higher. The monopolistic model plays down the international movement of capital and emphasizes the differences in the operations of local firms and foreign firms. The data in the next chapter are not consistent with either of these models. In the next chapter I compare firms' operating methods by looking at capital-labor ratios, wages, propensities to export and to import, value added as a proportion of sales, and rates of growth of output. The foreign firms in my sample do not bring much capital to the developing nations nor, in general, do they operate very differently from the local firms.

The competitive model assumes that knowledge is instantaneously transmitted in all directions once the foreign firms arrive: the foreign firms immediately learn about operating in the local economy, and the local firms immediately absorb the foreigners' technology and management skills. The monopoly model assumes the foreign firm quickly learns about the local economy while it prevents the local firms from acquiring its skills. I look at these questions in the next chapter by examining how rapidly firms attain maximum productivity levels and how many persons who work for local firms have previously been employed by foreign firms.

THEORETICAL MODELS OF PERFECT COMPETITION

On the one hand, I think it would be folly to come to any startling conclusions on the basis of so simplified a model and such abstract reasoning; but on the other hand, strong simple cases often point the way to an element of truth present in a complex situation.

Paul A. Samuelson

This supplement is a theoretical critique of the standard competitive model for evaluating the impact of foreign investment. I begin by assuming, following the standard model, that each firm acts as a perfect competitor and maximizes profits in a world of perfect certainty. I then depart from the standard model by examining the impact of foreign firms that bring a new technology and additional capital. I then introduce the further complications that foreigners invest in only part of the economy and also bring better management skills.

The possibility that foreign firms may bring an inappropriate technology may be graphically illustrated for a one-sector economy by slightly modifying MacDougall's approach. Assume perfect competition in the host country, full employment, and no taxes on profits earned by foreign investors (as argued in chapters 3 and 4, this is a realistic assumption about taxes for firms exporting manufactures). Suppose that initially all capital is owned locally and the amount of capital in the host country is *oa*. Then in diagram 2.1 total output (and national income) is the area under the marginal productivity of capital curve MPK_I and the rate of profit is *oc*. Now suppose *ab* of foreign capital enters the country. With no change in technology, the marginal product of capital falls in the host country to *oj*. National income increases; the income of local workers increases, and the income of local capitalists falls. This is the essence of MacDougall's analysis.

But suppose the foreign capital brings along a new technology which tilts the marginal productivity of capital curve to MPK_{II}. The equilibrium rate of profit rises to *od*, and total output is the area under the new marginal productivity of capital curve (*oehb*), which may well be larger than the old total product (*ofga*). But now foreigners receive some of this larger output: the profit rate times the amount of foreign capital (or the rectangle *abhi*). So

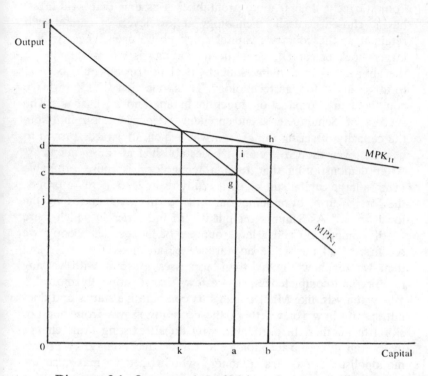

Diagram 2.1. Output and Capital in a One-Sector Model

national income with foreign capital may be smaller than without foreign capital; it is an empirical matter of comparing *ofga* with *oehb* minus *abhi*. Even if the host country taxes some of the profits earned by the foreign investors, national income with the foreign investment may be less than it was without the foreign investment.

In diagram 2.1, foreign technology is more profitable than domestic technology at the initial level of capital, is not used by local capitalists prior to the arrival of foreign investors, and then is used by all local capitalists after foreigners arrive. How might one rationalize this assumed sequence? First, one notes that with small amounts of capital (any amount less than *ok* in diagram 2.1) domestic technology is more profitable.[57] I assume that local firms, having chosen domestic technology at low levels of capital, will retain it as the country's capital stock grows even when, with a larger stock of capital, domestic technology is less profitable. In the absence of foreign investment, local managers could be said to forget about foreign technology. Thus, one views the knowledge contained in a production function in an innovative sense. The success of Schumpeter's entrepreneur "depends upon intuition, the capacity of seeing things in a way which afterwards proves to be true, even though it cannot be established at the moment." [58] After demonstrating that foreign technology is more profitable (with a large capital stock) by actually using it to increase profits, the foreign firm, by assumption, will be quickly imitated by the local firms.[59] As Schumpeter put it, "In industries in which there is still competition and a large number of independent people we see first of all the single appearance of an innovation . . . and then we see how the existing businesses grasp it with varying rapidity and completeness, first a few, then continually more." [60]

My analysis, like MacDougall's, is comparative statics and does not specify how (or whether) the economy moves from one position to another. In particular, why do all existing firms change over from domestic technology to foreign technology? A private monopolistic (or central planner) who wished to maximize the income of all capitalists would have some plants continue using domestic technology. My argument simply demonstrates that if

57. One could, of course, have foreign technology be more profitable for any amount of capital. Then total output with foreign technology will always be greater than with domestic technology.

58. Joseph A. Schumpeter, *The Theory of Economy Development* (Oxford: Oxford University Press paperback, 1961), p. 85.

59. In this model there are no distortions in factor prices. In the real world foreign firms may earn larger profits because they pay less for some inputs; monopolistic practices may prevent local firms from imitating foreign firms.

60. Schumpeter, *Theory of Economic Development*, p. 229.

all firms, local and foreign, behave in the same way, then foreign investment may reduce host country income.

It may be useful to illustrate this argument with a numerical example. Suppose the domestic production function is

$$O = 1.16 \, L^{1/2} K^{1/2} \tag{2.1}$$

where O = output, L = stock of labor, and K = stock of capital. Suppose the foreign production function is

$$O = L^{1/4} K^{3/4} \tag{2.2}$$

Thus both production functions are assumed to belong to the Cobb-Douglas family.

Assume full employment, profit rate, π, equal to the marginal productivity of capital, MPK, and the wage rate W, equal to the marginal productivity of labor, MPL. Suppose that initially there are 100 units of labor and 64 units of local domestic capital.

As shown in column 1 of table 2.2, output with domestic tech-

Table 2.2. Alternative Production Functions and Foreign Investment

	Domestic technology (Output is $1.16 \, L^{1/2} K^{1/2}$)			Foreign technology (Output is $L^{1/4} K^{1/4}$)		
	(1)	(2)	(3)	(4)	(5)	(6)
Labor stock	100	100	100	100	100	100
Capital stock ·	64	100	25	64	100	25
Output	92.80	116	58	71.6	100	35.36
Profit rate	.725	.58	1.16	.839	.75	1.061
Wage rate	.464	.58	.29	.179	.25	.088
Capital's income	46.4	58	29	53.7	75	26.52
Labor's income	46.4	58	29	17.9	25	8.84
Foreign capital's income	0	20.88	0	0	27	0
Local capital's income	46.40	37.12	29	53.7	48	26.52
National income	92.80	95.12	58	71.6	73	35.36

nology is 92.80, the profit rate is .725, and the local capitalists receive 46.40. Suppose that 36 units of foreign capital are added to the domestic capital. Using domestic technology, output rises (column 2) to 116 and the rate of profit falls to .58. As foreign capitalists earn 20.88 ($.58 \times 36 = 20.88$), national income is 95.12 ($116 - 20.88 = 95.12$). If all firms shift to foreign technology, then output (column 5) is 100—more than in the absence of foreign capital but less than using foreign capital and domestic technology. The profit rate using foreign technology is .75, higher than with domestic technology (and the wage rate is lower with the foreign technology). National income is 73 $(100 - .75 \times 36 = 73)$, which is less than if foreign capital were combined with domestic technology and also less than in the complete absence of foreign capital.[61]

In a one-sector model, therefore, one need not explain a coalition between local capitalists and foreign capitalists solely on political grounds.[62] Even if foreigners behave as perfect competitors, it is theoretically possible for foreign capitalists to reduce the total income accruing to the natives, to increase the income accruing to local capitalists, and to reduce the income accruing to local workers.

I now consider a two-sector economy whose industries are agriculture and manufacturing, using two factors of production, labor and capital. At first glance this resembles a Heckscher-Ohlin model, where foreign investment is seen as a substitute for foreign trade.[63] But the Heckscher-Ohlin model assumes that production functions are the same throughout the world and that every businessman always maximizes profits. Let us relax these assumptions.

I suppose that each commodity, A and B, is produced by a Cobb-Douglas production function, and the quantities produced

61. Note that at a low level of domestic capital—say 25 units—the domestic technology is both more profitable (1.16 versus 1.061) and more productive (58 versus 35.36), as is shown by comparing columns 3 and 6.

62. Baran, for example, says, "Afraid that hostility toward foreign interests might deprive them of foreign support in a case of revolutionary emergency, the native capitalists deserted their previous anti-imperialist, nationalist platforms." Paul A. Baran, "On the Political Economy of Backwardness," *The Manchester School* 20 (January 1952), reprinted in *The Economics of Underdevelopment,* ed. A. N. Agarwala and S. P. Singh (Oxford: Oxford University Press paperback, 1958), p. 80.

63. See, for example, Robert Mundell, "International Trade and Factor Mobility," *American Economic Review* 47 (June 1957), reprinted in Caves and Johnson, *Readings in International Economics,* pp. 101–14. Ohlin, tempering formal logic with empirical observation, was more cautious. Observing that there were many factors at work, he concluded that "the tendency toward a reduction of trade may be counteracted by a tendency to increased trade." Ohlin, *Interregional and International Trade,* p. 215.

are valued at world prices (P_A and P_M).[64] Symbolically, let Q_i be the quantity of the *i*th good produced, and let L_i and K_i be the amounts of labor and capital used in the production of the *i*th good:

$$Q_A = L_A{}^\gamma K_A{}^{1-\gamma} \quad \text{where } 0 < \gamma < 1 \tag{2.3}$$

$$Q_M = L_M{}^B K_M{}^{1-B} \quad \text{where } 0 < B < 1 \tag{2.4}$$
$$\text{and } \gamma > B$$

The total supplies of labor, $\overline{L}$, and of capital, $\overline{K}$, are fixed and there is no open unemployment although, as discussed below, there is disguised unemployment. Thus:

$$L_A + L_M = \overline{L} \tag{2.5}$$

$$K_A + K_M = \overline{K} \tag{2.6}$$

Initially managers are assumed to lack a capitalist mentality: rather than maximize profits, they hire labor until the money wage rate, w_i, equals a fraction, f_i, of the average revenue product of labor in the sector. Capitalists also receive a rate of return, r_i, on the capital used in each sector. My model is thus somewhat related to Arthur Lewis's subsistence economy,[65] though in my model labor does not receive the entire agricultural product and the agricultural wage level is not set exogenously.[66] While labor

64. One can justify the use of world prices in two ways: (1) governments frequently announce, as an objective, achieving a certain level of real output over the next few years in "constant prices," which in practice either are the prices observed in some base period (set by the actual working of the economy) or are prices set by the government's planners (representing the planners' utility function); and (2) international trade theory shows how a society maximizes its utility by producing at the point on its transformation curve that maximizes its output valued at world prices and then trading at world prices to reach its highest indifference curve; for a small country world prices can be taken as exogenous.

65. W. Arthur Lewis, "Economic Development with Unlimited Supplies of Labour," *The Manchester School* 22 (May 1954): 139–91. See also John C. H. Fei and Gustav Ranis, *Development of the Labor Surplus Economy: Theory and Policy* (Homewood, Ill.: Richard D. Irwin, 1964); and Richard A. Brecher, "Disguised Versus Open Unemployment: A Trade-Off," mimeographed (New Haven, October 1971).

66. Unlike Lewis, I assume that both labor and capital are used in agriculture and that the capital/labor ratio is higher in manufacturing. For example, Ho presents data that indicate that in Taiwan in 1951 the capital/labor ratio of agriculture was about one-sixth that of nonagriculture. Ho

is paid a fraction of its average product, I do not assume labor's marginal product is zero.[67]

$$W_A = P_A f_A \left(\frac{K_A}{L_A}\right)^{1-\gamma} \qquad \text{where } 0 < f_A < 1 \qquad (2.7)$$

$$r_A = P_A(1 - f_A)\left(\frac{K_A}{L_A}\right)^{-\gamma} \qquad (2.8)$$

$$w_M = P_M f_M \left(\frac{K_M}{L_M}\right)^{1-B} \qquad \text{where } 0 < f_M < 1 \qquad (2.9)$$

$$r_M = p_M(1 - f_M)\left(\frac{K_M}{L_M}\right)^{-B} \qquad (2.10)$$

I assume capitalists and laborers move capital and labor around until money wage rates and interest rates are equal in both sectors:[68]

$$w_M = w_A \qquad (2.11)$$
$$r_M = r_A \qquad (2.12)$$

I also assume the country is so small that its output does not affect the world prices of the two goods. For simplicity, I let $P_A = P_M = 1$. When there are no foreigners in the country, output, Y, equals national income, NI.

$$Y = P_A Q_A + P_M Q_M = Q_A + Q_M \qquad (2.13)$$
$$Y = NI \qquad (2.14)$$

Once we stipulate the total amount of capital, the total amount of labor, and the fraction of the average product which workers

---

says the wage in agriculture in Taiwan is set by the average product of labor in agriculture. Yhi-Min Ho, "Development with Surplus Population— The Case of Taiwan: A Critique of the Classical Two-Sector Model, à la Lewis," *Economic Development and Cultural Change* 20 (January 1972): 212, 213, 224.

67. Little, Scitovsky, and Scott conclude, "There is now a wide consensus of opinion that this marginal product [of labor in agriculture] is significantly greater than zero even in the most overpopulated countries such as India and Pakistan." Ian Little, Tibor Scitovsky, and Maurice Scott, *Industry and Trade in Some Developing Countries: A Comparative Study* (London: Oxford University Press paperback, 1970), p. 146.

68. In Lewis's model, the wage rate is higher in the modern sector. This assumption could be stated by slightly modifying equation 2.11 to be

$$w_M = k w_A, \text{ where } k > 1 \qquad (2.11')$$

receive as a wage rate in each sector, we can solve this system of twelve equations describing a precapitalist economy.

Now suppose a group of foreigners arrives, bringing additional capital, FK, a capitalist mentality, and new technology.[69] Their sole objective is to maximize profits, but I assume there is a competitive environment.[70] As noted in chapter 2, foreign capitalists tend to invest in only part of the economy. Assume that foreigners invest in manufacturing and that all capitalists in the manufacturing sector thereupon become competitive profit maximizers; they therefore all hire labor until its marginal revenue product equals the money wage rate. In the agriculture sector labor is still hired until its money wage equals a fraction of its average revenue product.[71] A mixed economy now exists.

As foreigners invest only in manufacturing, the new technology is confined to manufacturing, and so equation 2.4 becomes

$$Q_M = L_M{}^{B'} K_M{}^{1-B'} \qquad 0 < B' < 1 \tag{2.4$'$}$$

What will happen to national income (total output less profits earned by the foreigners on their capital)? A quick answer might be that since at least some firms are behaving rationally (maximizing profits) and since the capital stock is larger, national income will rise in a fashion analogous to MacDougall's analysis of a one-sector economy. But there is a new technology and also the possibility of a second-best situation, since only the manufacturing sector maximizes profits. Thus, in this new mixed economy equations 2.9 and 2.10 are replaced by:

---

69. While I use the word "technology," the foreign company might bring new methods which affect the productivity of labor. For example, the company might change the workers' loyalty to the company. For a brief discussion of Japanese techniques for affecting workers' productivity, see Ezra Vogel, "The Social Base of Japan's Postwar Economic Growth," in *United States International Economic Policy in an Interdependent World: Papers Submitted to the Commission on International Trade and Investment Policy* (Washington, D.C.: U.S. Government Printing Office, 1971), 2: 135–38, 149–50.

70. As Little, Scitovsky, and Scott put it, foreign capitalists "manifest greater reliance on careful calculations of costs and profitability than is customary in developing countries." Little, Scitovsky, and Scott, *Industry and Trade*, p. 57.

71. So agriculture may include some small-scale rural manufacturing.

$$w_M = P_M B' \left(\frac{K_M}{L_M}\right)^{1-B'} \tag{2.9'}$$

$$r_M = p_M(1 - B') \left(\frac{K_M}{L_M}\right)^{-B'} \tag{2.10'}$$

As the capital stock is larger, equation 2.6 is replaced by:

$$K_A + K_M = \overline{K} + FK \tag{2.6'}$$

National income is less than output because of the income of foreign capitalists, and so equation 2.14 is replaced by:

$$NI = Y - r_M FK \tag{2.14'}$$

While I do not have a general solution for this system of equations, for specific sets of parameters I can compare the precapitalist system with the mixed system. For both the precapitalist and mixed economies I let $\gamma = .8$ and $P_A = P_M = 1$; B is .2 in the precapitalist society, and initially the capital stock is 100, the labor stock is 100, $f_A = .90$, and $f_M = .30$.[72]

With these parameter values, both output and national income in the precapitalist economy are 117.09.[73] Now suppose the for-

72. A partial equilibrium approach might suggest that the wage rate is higher in the precapitalist economy than it would be if all firms maximized profits. In agriculture, for example, the average product of labor is $\left(\frac{K_A}{L_A}\right)^{.2}$, and so the agricultural wage is .9 $\left(\frac{K_A}{L_A}\right)^{.2}$. If labor were paid its marginal product, the agricultural wage would be .8 $\left(\frac{K_A}{L_A}\right)^{.2}$. However, the general equilibrium solution indicates that the wage rate in the precapitalist economy is .58, which is less than the equilibrium wage rate of .61 when all firms maximize profits.

73. With these parameter values and all firms maximizing profits, output and national income are 121.26. Output would be increased by 3 percent if all firms maximized profits. While this increase may seem small to those noneconomists who remember that most national economies grow by at least 5 percent per annum, it is large compared to other estimates of the losses in output due to static inefficiencies. Dougherty and Selowsky estimate a maximum loss in output of 2 percent in Colombia due to wage distortions, and they cite six other studies showing losses in output of less than 1 percent due to either monopoly or tariffs. Christopher Dougherty and Marcelo Selowsky, "Measuring the Effects of the Misallocation of Labor," *Review of Economics and Statistics* 55 (August 1973): pp. 386–90. Given these studies, why do academic economists continue to spend so much time teaching (preaching?) about the evils of distortions?

eigners bring ten units of capital ($FK = 10$), all manufacturing
firms maximize profits, and B becomes .4. Thus the foreigners
bring a technology to manufacturing that is more labor-intensive
than the one the native manufacturing firms initially used.[74] Then
output in the mixed economy falls to 111.20 and national income
is 106.71. The rate of return on capital falls from .59 to .45, and
the wage rate rises from .58 to .62.[75] These results are sum-
marized in columns 1 and 4 of table 2.3.

What is the economic story behind these results? The impact
of the foreigners can be divided into three parts: a change in the
allocation of labor and local capital because of a change in the
behavior of manufacturing firms; an increase in the stock of
capital; and a change in the allocation of labor and capital because of the new manufacturing technology.

Changing the mentality of all manufacturers leads them to
change the capital/labor ratio; with my parameters the capital/
labor ratio in manufacturing rises from 2.26 in the precapitalist
economy to 3.71 in the mixed economy and falls slightly in agriculture, from .108 to .103. The wage rate is lower, and the interest
rate is higher. Money costs are higher in manufacturing and output of manufacturing contracts. As both labor and capital shift
into agriculture, the value of the extra agricultural output is more
than the value of the lost manufacturing output, and so the value
of total output rises by about one percent, from 117.09 to
118.68.[76] This result can be seen by comparing columns 1 and 2
in table 2.3.

The effect of increasing the stock of capital from 100 to 110,
given the change in behavior, is to reduce the output of agri-

74. The new technology is more labor-intensive in the sense that for a
given ratio of wage rate to interest rate a profit-maximizing firm would
have a higher ratio of labor to capital.
75. While this section does not deal with domestic savings, the distribution of income is obviously important for future total income if the
marginal propensity to save of workers differs from that of capitalists.
76. It is even possible for the change in mentality to reduce the value
of output. Consider a case where $P_A = 3.0$ and $P_M = 1.0$. Then for the
precapitalist parameters shown in column 1 of table 2.3, the value of domestic income is 290.6. Introducing profit-maximizing behavior in manufacturing reduces domestic income to 289.9, as agricultural output rises from
90.11 to 90.13 and manufacturing output falls from 20.28 to 19.53.

Table 2.3. Foreign Investment in a Two-Sector Model

	Precapitalist		Mixed	
	(1)	(2)	(3)	(4)
Labor ($\bar{L}$)	100	100	100	100
Capital ($\bar{K}$)	100	100	100	100
Foreign capital (FK)	0	0	10	10
Labor share in agriculture (f_A)	.9	.9	.9	.9
Labor share in manufacturing (f_M)	.3			
Agricultural output (Q_A)	37.51	47.73	45.97	34.71
Manufacturing output (Q_M)	79.58	70.95	78.86	76.49
Total output (Y)	117.09	118.68	124.83	111.20
National income (NI)	117.09	118.68	118.68	106.71
Interest rate (r)	.59	.62	.62	.45
Wage rate (w)	.58	.57	.57	.62
Capital/labor ratio:				
Agriculture	.108	.103	.103	.15
Manufacturing	2.26	3.71	3.71	2.07
Exponent on labor in Cobb-Douglas:				
Agriculture	.8	.8	.8	.8
Manufacturing	.2	.2	.2	.4

culture and to increase the output of manufactures, but the entire increase in total output (from 118.68 to 124.83) is absorbed by the foreign capitalists, and so national income remains at 118.68; this result can be seen by comparing columns 2 and 3 in table 2.3.

The effect of introducing the more labor-intensive technology in the entire manufacturing sector,[77] given the change in behavior and the increase in capital, is to lower the capital/labor ratio in manufacturing to 20.07 and to raise it to .15 in agriculture. The wage rate increases and the interest rate falls; output falls in both sectors. Total output falls from 124.83 to 111.20, and national income falls by ten percent, from 118.68 to 106.71. These results can be seen by comparing columns 3 and 4 in table 2.3.

The models presented in this supplement are a formal statement illustrating the importance of technology—in either a one-sector model or a two-sector model—in assessing the impact of foreign investors in terms of both the total size of national income

77. For evidence that foreign and local firms in manufacturing have about the same capital/labor ratios, see chapter 3.

and its distribution between labor and domestic capital. Depending on the type of technology brought by foreigners, foreign investment may either increase or reduce wages and may not increase national income.

SUPPLEMENT 2.2

EVIDENCE ON FOREIGN INVESTMENT
AND INSTABILITY

Econometrics is a way of studying history.
Lawrence Klein

Measuring the extent to which U.S. firms have overseas operations is the major data problem in estimating the impact of foreign investment on a firm's global risk. I use two measures, both developed by others. Bruck and Lees examined the *Fortune* 500 largest industrial firms for 1965; using company reports for the most part, they examined each firm's foreign operations in terms of sales, profits, assets, employment, and production and then assigned a single ranking to each of 335 firms; they were unable to collect enough data to rank the remaining 165 firms.[78]

From the point of view of testing a diversification model, their data have the disadvantage of viewing the world as having only two areas: the United States and the rest of the world. Thus one cannot test, with their data, the presumption that it makes a difference whether a firm with half its operations in the United States has operations in only one foreign country or in many foreign countries. I therefore also used the number of foreign countries in which in 1967 there was a manufacturing subsidiary owned by one of the 1963 *Fortune* 500 or the 1964 *Fortune* 500.[79]

The two major conceptual problems are identifying the variable that management wishes to maximize and measuring the risk attached to this variable. I find the discussion on whether management maximizes sales or profits after taxes to be inconclusive, and therefore examine both for 1961–69.[80] Following Fisher and

78. Nicholas K. Bruck and Francis A. Lees, *Foreign Investment, Capital Controls, and the Balance of Payments,* New York University Institute of Finance Bulletin no. 48–49 (New York, 1968).
79. These unpublished data were kindly made available to me by the Harvard Multinational Enterprise Project.
80. Data on annual worldwide sales and worldwide profits after taxes are from *Moody's* and from *Standard and Poor's.* Accounting practices

Hall,[81] I use as one measure of risk the standard deviation of the deviations around a fitted trend line,[82] divided by the average value of the observations. I call this measure the adjusted standard error. I also measure risk by the coefficient of variation (the standard deviation of the observations divided by their average value). As in most empirical studies, I use a measure of observed instability as a proxy for the degree of ignorance about the future.

I follow the allocation by Bruck and Lees of each company to one of forty-two industries based on the three digit Standard Industrial Classification (SIC) code. I then limit my study to those twenty-two industries which have at least five firms (table 2.4). I use twenty-one dummy variables to identify these industries.

On the conjecture that a firm can increase its stability by producing many products, I use the product diversification index of the Harvard Multinational Enterprise Project. This index is the number of five-digit SIC category products manufactured in 1966 by each company. Finally, I use as an independent variable the size of the company, measured by either the average annual sales or the average annual profits, during 1961–69.

In summary, I conjecture that the instability of a company's profits or sales (1) is negatively related to its foreign activities, the number of products it produces, and its size, and (2) depends on the industry to which it belongs.

What should be the functional relationship? The relationship may be nonlinear, but its precise form depends on the underlying assumptions. Take, for example, the impact of firm size. If (i)

---

differ among large companies; I classified seven types of companies: those which include all subsidiaries or all significant subsidiaries, those which include all wholly owned subsidiaries, those which include all majority owned subsidiaries, those which include subsidiaries in some regions (e.g., in Canada), those which exclude foreign subsidiaries, those which fall into a miscellaneous category, and those which give no indication. I omitted from my sample those companies which definitely exclude foreign subsidiaries.

81. I. N. Fisher and G. R. Hall, "Risk and Corporate Rates of Return," *Quarterly Journal of Economics* 83 (February 1969): 79–92.

82. Let x_t = sales or profits in year t and t = year t. Then the trend is computed by least-squares estimation of log $x_t = a + t$ log $(1 + b)$. Those companies having occasional negative profits during the period are therefore omitted from the sample.

Table 2.4. Number of Firms in Each Industry

Industry	SIC number	Number of firm in sample
Dairy products	202	7
Canning fruits and vegetables	203	8
Grain mill products	204	6
Bakery products	205	5
Textile mill products	221	11
Paper and allied products	262	13
Chemicals	281	19
Drugs	283	12
Soaps, detergents, and cosmetics	284	6
Petroleum refining	291	21
Glass and glass products	321	5
Concrete, gypsum, and asbestos	326	5
Steel works and mills	331	13
Nonferrous metals	333	12
Miscellaneous fabricated metal products	349	5
Farm and construction machinery	352	11
Metal working machinery	354	5
Electrical equipment and apparatus	361	8
Communications equipment	366	8
Motor vehicles and parts	371	5
Aircraft and parts	372	10
Optical instruments	383	5
Total firms		200

each national market is of equal size for the firm, (ii) each national market has the same variance, and (iii) there is zero correlation among national markets, then the coefficient of variation for the firm's sales or profits declines by the ratio of $1/\sqrt{N}$ where N is the number of national markets.[83] While none of these assumptions will be correct for most U.S. firms, the example does suggest experimenting with nonlinear relationships. Horst's empirical work also supports the notion of a nonlinear relationship between firm size and propensity to invest abroad. Experimentation with the logarithm of size, the square of size, and the reciprocal of size indicated that the reciprocal of size gives the best fit for my data. The reciprocal of size also satisfies the theoretical

83. Scherer, *Industrial Market Structure*, p. 101.

notion that a firm's stability approaches an asymptote. In each regression I arrange the firms by size and report the Durbin-Watson statistic (table 2.5, column 8). Positive serial correlation remains only for the two ordinary least squares regressions for the coefficient of variation of profits.

There is also the econometric problem of simultaneity. Grabowski and Mueller[84] suggest that U.S. firms with higher variability in earnings pay out larger dividends in order that management not be fired by dissident stockholders; firms with more stable earnings would have more retained earnings and so could undertake more foreign investment. I will shortly present some macro and industry evidence on the direction of causality; at this point I consider the possibility that overseas investment and stability are jointly determined and use two-stage least squares. I rely on Horst's work, which is the principal econometric study of foreign investment at the firm level. After considering the extent of vertical integration, labor or capital intensity, advertising or research effort, and product diversity, he concludes that "once inter-industry differences are washed out, the only influence of any separate significance is firm size." [85]

To summarize symbolically, let firm stability $= ST$, firm size $= S$, foreign investment $= FI$, number of products $= P$, industry dummies $= I_i$, and disturbance terms $= u$ and v. Then for ordinary least squares (OLS) the regression takes the form of:

$$ST = a + b_1FI + b_2P + \frac{b_3}{S} + \sum_{i=1}^{21} c_iI_i + u \qquad (2.15)$$

For two-stage least squares (2SLS):

$$ST = a_1 + b_1FI + b_2P + \sum_{i=1}^{21} c_iI_i + u \qquad (2.16)$$

$$FI = a_2 + \frac{b_3}{S} + \sum_{i=1}^{21} c_iI_i + v \qquad (2.17)$$

84. Henry C. Grabowski and Dennis C. Mueller, "Managerial and Stockholder Welfare Models of Firm Expenditures," *Review of Economics and Statistics* 54 (February 1972): 9–24.

85. Thomas Horst, "Firm and Industry Determinants of the Decision to Invest Abroad: An Empirical Study," *Review of Economics and Statistics* 54 (August 1972): 261.

Table 2.5. Instability of 200 Firms in the 1960s
(T ratios in parentheses)

	Constant (1)	Number of countries (2)	Overseas activity (3)	Number of products (4)	$\frac{1}{Size}$ (5)	R^2 (6)	F (7)	D-W (8)
Profits								
Coefficient of variation								
OLS	8.14 (4.07)	−.39 (−6.71)		−.02 (−.81)	−34.2 (−7.52)	.45	5.97	1.40
2SLS	2.92 (1.14)	.15 (1.11)		−.05 (−1.62)		.10	.82	1.22
OLS	13.21 (6.54)		−.02 (−8.90)	−.05 (−2.49)	−37.2 (−8.73)	.52	8.03	1.38
2SLS	.50 (.15)		.01 (1.40)	−.05 (−1.63)		−.004	−.03	1.31
Adjusted standard error								
OLS	.001 (.02)	−.0001 (−.13)		−.0001 (−.32)	.39 (5.19)	.27	2.71	2.27
2SLS	.05 (1.46)	−.01 (−2.53)		.0001 (.21)		.10	.84	2.08
OLS	.002 (.06)		−.00001 (−.15)	−.0001 (−.36)	.39 (5.15)	.27	2.71	2.27
2SLS	.12 (2.55)		−.0003 (−3.00)	−.0002 (−.45)		.03	.24	2.22

Sales

Coefficient of
variation

OLS	.55 (7.46)	−.01 (−2.45)		−.0004 (−.53)	−13.8 (−2.20)	.23	2.23	1.94
2SLS	.48 (6.81)	−.002 (−.45)		−.0001 (.14)		.21	2.03	1.87
OLS	.51 (6.20)		−.00002 (−.17)	−.001 (−1.11)	−7.81 (−1.25)	.21	1.92	1.87
2SLS	.43 (4.83)		.0001 (.70)	−.001 (−.81)		.20	1.86	1.87

Adjusted
standard error

OLS	.0001 (1.26)	−.00001 (−1.48)		−.000000 (−.33)	.07 (7.20)	.48	6.85	2.10
2SLS	.001 (4.28)	−.00004 (−5.38)		.000000 (.19)		.17	1.61	2.06
OLS	.0001 (.98)		−.000000 (−.45)	−.000001 (−.67)	.07 (7.80)	.48	6.69	2.07
?SLS	.001 (5.07)		−.000002 (−4.53)	−.000003 (−1.73)		.06	.46	2.00

Data limitations reduce my sample size to 200 firms. Table 2.5 gives the results for 2.15 and 2.16 for 1961–69 for all variables except the dummy variables. Since I look at two measures of risk and both sales and profits, there are four possible dependent variables. For each dependent variable there are two measures of foreign investment: the number of countries, and the Bruck and Lees ranking of overseas activity. Thus there are eight ordinary least squares regressions and eight two-stage least-squares regressions.[86]

Look first at the ordinary least squares results. Each regression is significant at the one percent level. The regressions explain from 21 to 52 percent of the variation in the relevant dependent variable. The number of countries variable (column 2) is significant in both regressions for the coefficient of variation, and the Bruck and Lees measure (column 3) is significant for the coefficient of variation of profits.[87] All eight equations have the predicted negative sign for each of the two measures of foreign investment. The number of products (column 4) has the predicted negative coefficient in all the equations, but is significant only in regression 3. The reciprocal of size (column 5) is significant in seven of the regressions but has a negative coefficient, rather than the expected positive one,[88] in the four regressions for the coefficient of variation.

Now look at the two-stage least squares results. As the R^2 was usually negative[89] in preliminary attempts to estimate equation 2.16, I created twenty-one additional instrumental variables to use in the first stage of the estimation.[90] In four of the eight regressions there is a significant negative coefficient on foreign investment. The R^2 for equation 2.16 is always lower than the R^2

86. All regressions were done using the Economic Growth Center Time Series Processor developed by Thomas Birnberg.

87. In this paragraph and the next two, a significant coefficient means one whose t ratio has an absolute value greater than 2.0.

88. If one expects instability to decrease with firm size, one expects it to increase with the reciprocal of firm size.

89. Since the R^2 is calculated using the original values of foreign investment, the second regression in two-stage least squares, which uses the predicted values of foreign investment, can yield a negative R^2.

90. In the notation of equations 2.16 and 2.17, instrumental variable $i = PI_i$.

for the corresponding regression for equation 2.15. These results may reflect the lack of a good equation for predicting overseas investment rather than a high degree of simultaneity. Depending on the definitions of foreign investment and size, the ordinary least squares regression for equation 2.17 yields values of R^2 ranging from .41 to .50. A satisfactory econometric solution to simultaneity must await a better model for predicting foreign investment by firms.[91] One could also do additional econometric experiments, such as trying more complicated functions or using different functions for each industry.

To summarize the econometric results: in thirteen of the sixteen regressions foreign investment has a negative coefficient, and seven of these coefficients are significant. By comparison, the number of products, which has received much professional attention as a way of increasing a firm's stability, has only one significant negative coefficient. I focus on the seven significant negative coefficients for foreign investment. The number of countries has a significant negative coefficient in four cases, as compared with three for the Bruck and Lees measure. Profits has four significant negative coefficients, as compared with three for sales. The coefficient of variation has three significant negative coefficients as compared with four for the adjusted standard error. Ordinary least squares has three significant negative coefficients, as compared with four for two-stage least squares.

There are two reasons why I do not believe that, for these data, a firm's foreign investment is a function of a firm's stability. First, recall that foreign investment is measured in 1965 or 1967; stability is measured from 1961 to 1969. Given the time lags in firms' decision making and implementation, I find it implausible that in such a short time stability could have much influence on foreign investment. Second, there is evidence, to which I now turn, that different national markets are not perfectly correlated and so foreign investment could have increased a firm's stability in the 1960s.

To illustrate the correlations among various economies, I concentrate on GNP in current prices in Australia, Brazil, Canada,

91. One could also increase the R^2 by creating additional instrumental variables.

France, Germany, and the United Kingdom. These six countries accounted for 70 percent of the book value of all foreign U.S. investments in manufacturing in 1970.[92] I convert GNP in local currency and current prices to dollars, on the assumption that U.S. firms use dollars as the unit of account. Occasional large devaluations of foreign exchange rates are more than offset by inflation and by growth in real GNP in each of these countries, so that in the 1960s the dollar value of foreign GNP increased in almost every year. I therefore estimate the trend value of the aggregate dollar GNP of these six countries and the United States from 1960 to 1969; the trend in the annual rate of growth for these seven countries is 7.4 percent. I then calculate the deviations from this "world" trend for each country in each year. For France the actual rate of growth always exceeds 7.4 percent; for the United Kingdom the actual rate is always less than 7.4 percent; for the other five countries the actual annual rate is sometimes more than 7.4 percent and sometimes less. I then calculate the correlations among these annual national deviations from the "world" trend.

The results are shown in table 2.6. Consider a company whose

Table 2.6. Correlations of Deviations from
Average "World" GNP, 1961–69

	U.S.	Australia	Brazil	Canada	U.K.	Germany	France
U.S.	1.00	−.71	.64	.64	−.55	.44	.28
Australia		1.00	−.95	−.88	.85	−.36	−.75
Brazil			1.00	.87	−.82	.47	.71
Canada				1.00	−.84	.60	.84
U.K.					1.00	−.33	−.73
Germany						1.00	.30
France							1.00

Source: GNP in current prices and in national currency and exchange rates from various issues of *International Financial Statistics* (Washington, D.C.: International Monetary Fund).

main orientation is toward the United States; deviations of U.S. GNP from the world trend are negatively correlated with GNP

92. *Survey of Current Business,* October 1971, p. 33.

deviations in Australia and the United Kingdom and have a correlation of less than .65 with GNP deviations in the other four countries. To the extent that industry sales or profits are correlated with GNP, this evidence supports the view that overseas investment leads to more stability about the world trend.

If there were differences among industries in the extent to which national markets are correlated, this could help explain the large differences in foreign investment among industries which were noted in chapter 2. (Comparable data on industries in various countries are so fragmentary that the following analysis is, at best, suggestive.) Consider, for example, leather (ISIC 29) and electrical machinery (ISIC 37). Vernon's 187 multinational firms account for 14 percent of U.S. sales of the leather industry and 50 percent of U.S. sales of the electrical machinery industry. Comparable data are available for annual industry sales[93] from 1963 through 1967 for the United States, Australia, Canada, and Germany. I follow the same procedure as for GNP. For each industry I convert national industry sales to dollars at the current exchange rate, aggregate the national sales to get "world" sales, compute the trend in world sales, calculate the deviations in each national industry's sales from the world trend, and then compute the correlations among the national deviations. The results for these two industries are shown in table 2.7. Canadian deviations from the world trend are about equally correlated with U.S. deviations in both industries; for Australia and Germany deviations are more highly correlated with U.S. deviations for the leather industry than for the electrical machinery industry. Thus, as implied by the theory, the industry that had a greater correlation among national markets in the mid-1960s, and thus less scope for reducing global risk by foreign investment, had relatively fewer multinational firms in the mid-1960s. While one could extend this analysis to other industries, a more sophisticated analysis awaits better data on industry sales and profits in various countries.

In conclusion, both regression analysis and correlations among national markets support the hypothesis that large U.S. corpora-

93. Data on profits are unavailable.

Table 2.7. Correlations of Deviations from
Average "World" Sales, 1963–67

	U.S.	Australia	Canada	Germany
Leather				
U.S.	1.00	−.11	.78	.82
Australia		1.00	−.50	.39
Canada			1.00	.31
Germany				1.00
Electrical machinery				
U.S.	1.00	−.87	.85	−.53
Australia		1.00	−.55	.81
Canada			1.00	−.01
Germany				1.00

Sources: National sales in local currency from *The Growth of World Industry: 1968 Edition*, vol. 1 (New York: United Nations, 1970). Exchange rates from *International Financial Statistics.*

tions with more extensive foreign activities tended to have smaller fluctuations in global profits and sales in the 1960s. This result does not, of course, allow one to conclude that U.S. firms invested in foreign countries in order to reduce their risks. Reducing risk (or increasing sales or profits) may be the unintended result of corporate actions taken for other reasons.

3

Case Studies

*I pass with relief from the tossing sea of Cause and Theory
to the firm ground of Result and Fact.*

Winston Churchill

The previous chapter suggested that those theories which are the
most mathematically elegant and lead to the most precise conclusions about the consequences of foreign investment are the ones
which are forced to ignore most of the broad facts about foreign
investment;[1] furthermore, as demonstrated in supplement 2.1, a
slight shift in assumptions can lead to a complete reversal of the
conclusions about the impact of foreign investment on the size and
distribution of national income. Those theories that are most
consistent with the broad facts of private foreign investment are
least able to give precise conclusions about its consequences.

Nor can one gain much guidance on the impact of foreign investment by turning to previous empirical work on developing
countries. As the Pearson Commission said in 1969, "In the
absence of detailed empirical studies, it is difficult to pass a defini-
tive verdict on the precise size of the contribution which foreign
investment has made to development."[2] Vernon, discussing the

1. As Caves and Jones put it, "An understanding of the causes and
effects of direct investment is best gained by leaving the simple general-
equilibrium models, usually so helpful in international economics, and
turning to models . . . of imperfect competition and the analysis of technological factors." Richard E. Caves and Ronald W. Jones, *World Trade
and Payments: An Introduction* (Boston: Little, Brown and Co., 1973),
p. 487. Since, as noted in chapter 2, the same U.S. firms which make
most U.S. foreign investments also engage in a large share of U.S. foreign
trade, one wonders why foreign trade is not analyzed in terms of imperfect competition.

2. *Partners in Development: Report of the Commission on International
Development* (New York: Praeger, 1969), p. 104.

extent to which foreign firms introduce into developing countries production techniques that are excessively capital intensive, says that "the actual facts are, as usual, obscure. There are no comprehensive data on the degree to which multinational enterprises adapt their production processes to the conditions of less-developed countries, and scarcely any data at all on the comparative adaptive actions of local competitors." [3] The lack of empirical evidence did not, it might be noted, prevent the Pearson Commission from concluding that "foreign investment has contributed greatly to the growth of developing countries and can do even more in the future." [4]

The rest of this chapter presents the results of my study of twenty-seven U.S. and Japanese firms and nineteen local firms in South Korea, Taiwan, and Singapore. Since I discuss common problems of data collection and interpretation only in the section on South Korea, readers especially interested in either Singapore or Taiwan should at least skim the discussion of South Korea.

GENERAL COMPARISON OF SOUTH KOREA, SINGAPORE, AND TAIWAN

Whether one sees differences or similarities in a comparison depends on one's standards. Compared with India's 538 million people, the populations of South Korea, Taiwan, and Singapore all seem small. Yet South Korea has 32 million people, more than twice Taiwan's 14 million persons and more than fifteen times Singapore's 2 million persons. All three of these countries[5] were colonies until after World War II, Singapore being ruled by the British and Taiwan and South Korea by the Japanese. The current political boundaries of all three countries are of recent origin. South Korea was separated from North Korea after World War II; Taiwan's political connections with mainland China

3. Raymond Vernon, *Sovereignty at Bay: The Multinational Spread of U.S. Enterprises* (New York: Basic Books, 1971), p. 181.

4. *Partners in Development*, p. 99.

5. Throughout this chapter I refer to the Republic of Korea as South Korea and the Republic of China as Taiwan. I also refer to Taiwan as a country although both the Republic of China and the People's Republic of China refer to Taiwan as a province of China.

ceased in 1949. Singapore was an almost deserted island until 1819; it became part of the Federation of Malaysia in 1963 and became a separate independent nation in 1965.

In all three countries practically all young people have completed elementary school. All three had a rapid growth in real per capita GNP in the 1960s: 5.2 percent per annum for Singapore, 6.8 percent per annum for South Korea, and 7.1 percent per annum for Taiwan. The annual rate of population growth in the 1960s was 2.4 percent for Singapore, 2.6 percent for South Korea, and 2.9 percent for Taiwan.[6] Casual observation suggests that living standards in all three countries are well above that of a developing country like India. The World Bank estimates per capita GNP in 1970 at $920 in Singapore, $390 in Taiwan, and $250 in South Korea, as compared with about $110 in India.[7] Exports are a large fraction of GNP for all three nations: about one-sixth for South Korea, one-third for Taiwan, and four-fifths for Singapore. The annual rate of inflation between 1963 and 1970, as measured by changes in the consumer price index, was 1.2 percent in Singapore, 2.8 percent in Taiwan, and 13.9 percent in South Korea.[8]

All three countries passed laws in the 1960s that were designed to attract private foreign investment.[9] The broad features of these laws are similar: exemption for five years from taxes on profits, duty free import of capital equipment and of materials which are used in exported commodities, and no restrictions on either the percentage of equity that the foreign firm can own or on the amount of profits it can repatriate.

Relying heavily on entrepôt trade, Singapore has a history of low tariffs and few administrative controls on imports and ex-

6. Data on the growth of real per capita GNP and of population are from *The World Bank Atlas,* as reported in "The World Bank Atlas: Population, Growth Rate, and GNP Tables," *Finance and Development* 10 (March 1973): 26–27.

7. Ibid.

8. Data from *International Financial Statistics* (Washington, D.C.: International Monetary Fund, 1973), pp. 312, 88, 224.

9 Taiwan enacted the Statute for Encouragement of Investment in 1960 and revised it in 1965. South Korea's Foreign Capital Inducement Law was enacted in 1966. Singapore's Economic Expansion Incentives (Relief from Income Tax) Act was passed in 1967.

ports. South Korea and Taiwan, on the other hand, both have high import duties and government licensing of most imports. In the late 1950s and early 1960s Taiwan liberalized its foreign trade by devaluing its exchange rate, changing its tariffs, and gradually eliminating licensing for many imports; South Korea adopted a similar package of policy changes in the mid-1960s.[10] Both countries still have licensing of imports; for example, in 1970 South Korea had 719 items whose imports were automatically approved, 520 items for which individual import licenses were necessary, and 73 items whose imports were prohibited; in 1970 Taiwan had 7,239 items for which imports were licensed liberally, 4,127 items for which imports were licensed restrictively, and 209 items whose import was prohibited.[11]

Perhaps because of these import policies, Taiwan established an export zone at Kaohsiung in 1966, and South Korea established an export zone outside Seoul in the late 1960s. Firms located in these export zones agree to export their entire output and receive

10. Both countries also introduced changes in monetary and fiscal policy. For a discussion of some of the short-term economic consequences of these changes in South Korea, see Benjamin I. Cohen and Gustav Ranis, "The Second Postwar Restructuring," in *Government and Economic Development*, ed. Gustav Ranis, pp. 431–69 (New Haven: Yale University Press, 1971). For a discussion of the Taiwan case, see Ian Little, Tibor Scitovsky, and Maurice Scott, *Industry and Trade in Some Developing Countries, A Comparative Study* (London: Oxford University Press paperback, 1970), pp. 254–58, 388–89.

Neither study deals with the impact of trade liberalization on income distribution. The alleged reduction in income inequality in Taiwan is attributed by Little, Scitovsky, and Scott (p. 45) to the land reform of the 1950s. I say "alleged reduction" because Richard Weisskoff, who has looked at the basic data on Taiwan's income distribution, says that incomparability of the data preclude one's saying anything about the trend in income distribution.

A recent study of industrial concentration in 234 South Korean industries found a slight increase in concentration—measured by share of industry sales by the four or eight largest firms—between 1966 and 1969. How does one interpret this trend? Does the liberalization of a capitalist economy increase concentration or reduce it? The basic data on changes in industrial concentration are in Woo H. Nam, "Industry Concentration and Performance: Korean Manufacturing Industries" (Seoul: Korea Development Institute Working Paper 7209, June 1972).

11. The adverbs describing Taiwan's import policies and the general description of Taiwan's and South Korea's import policies are from *Twenty-Second Annual Report on Exchange Restrictions* (Washington, D.C.: International Monetary Fund, 1971), pp. 94, 253.

easy administrative access to imports. Not all exporters are located in these zones, for reasons such as proximity to the capital or lack of adequate land. In 1971, for example, exports from the Kaohsiung export zone were $156 million, or only 11 percent of Taiwan's total exports of manufactures.

FOREIGN FIRMS AND INDUSTRIAL EXPORTS

The specific incentives for foreign investors and general economic and political conditions in these three countries led to a large increase in foreign investment in the late 1960s. By the end of 1971 Taiwan's government had approved 631 foreign investments, with a total value of $521 million; 348 of these projects, with a total value of $369 million, were approved from 1968 through 1971. About 500 of these foreign enterprises were operating by the end of 1971.[12] The South Korean government approved 266 foreign projects through the end of 1970; these projects had a total foreign capital of $529 million, of which $214 million was equity and $315 million was foreign loans. The bulk of these South Korean projects—215 projects with an equity investment of $161 million—were approved from 1968 through 1970.[13] In Singapore there were only sixteen foreign manufacturing firms at the end of the 1950s. By the end of 1966 the government of Singapore had approved 136 foreign manufacturing firms, of which 91 were "Pioneer" (special privilege) firms;[14] by the end of 1971 the government had approved 110 foreign Pioneer firms.[15]

While the definitions of foreign investment are probably not identical, the data in table 3.1 suggest that the bulk of the foreign

12. *Foreign-Invested Enterprises in Taiwan, Republic of China* (Taipei: Council for International Economic Cooperation and Development, 1972), pp. 6, 7.

13. "Total Foreign Equity and Loan Funds Authorized for Projects Approved Under the Foreign Capital Inducement Law (FCIL) Since 1962," mimeographed (Seoul: U.S. Agency for International Development, 1971).

14. Helen Hughes and You Poh Seng, eds., *Foreign Investment and Industrialisation in Singapore* (Canberra: Australian National University Press, 1969), p. 178. I discuss Pioneer firms in more detail in the section on Singapore.

15. "Alphabetical List of Pioneer and Pioneer-in-Principle Establishments by Major Industry Group as at 31.12.1971," mimeographed (Singapore, 1972).

Table 3.1. Origin of Foreign Investments

	U.S.		Japan		Other	
	Number	Equity ($ million)	Number	Equity ($ million)	Number	Equity ($ million)
Taiwan	174	286	404	101	53	134
South Korea	96	128	144	57	26	29
Singapore	25	n.a.	13	n.a.	72	n.a.

Sources:
  Taiwan: Foreign-Invested Enterprises in Taiwan, p. 6.
  South Korea: "Foreign Equity and Loan Funds."
  Singapore: "Pioneer and Pioneer-in-Principle Establishments."

investment in Taiwan and South Korea is either U.S. or Japanese, with the average Japanese investment being smaller than the average U.S. investment. Singapore has overseas Chinese investment from Hong Kong, Indonesia, and Malaysia and also has investments by Australian and European companies.

Exports have grown rapidly in all three countries in recent years (table 3.2), with manufactured exports growing more rapidly than exports of other commodities. While petroleum and rubber still dominate Singapore's exports, in 1971 manufactures accounted for 71 percent of Taiwan's exports and 82 percent of South Korea's exports. Paauw and Fei have described Taiwan's economic performance since 1950 as a shift "from the land-based export system of colonialism to an export economy based upon labor efficiency and entrepreneurial ingenuity. . . . Taiwan shares this successful contemporary transition experience with few other countries, among which South Korea and Israel may be mentioned." [16]

Another perspective on the importance of manufactured exports from these countries can be acquired by looking at U.S. imports under tariff items 806.30 and 807.00.[17] In 1972 total imports by the U.S. from developing countries under these two tariff

16. Their study does not mention the role of foreign private investment in this transition. Douglas S. Paauw and John C. H. Fei, *The Transition in Open Dualistic Economies* (New Haven: Yale University Press, 1973), p. 93.
17. Items 806.30 and 807.00 concern the U.S. tariff on the foreign value added of U.S. imports of items fabricated from U.S. components.

Table 3.2. Exports of Taiwan, South Korea, and Singapore

| | Value (Millions of dollars) | | Annual |
	1967	1971	percentage change
Taiwan			
Manufactures[a]	394	1,428	38
Other	247	570	23
Total, Taiwan	641	1,998	33
South Korea			
Manufactures	214	875	42
Other	106	193	16
Total, South Korea	320	1,068	35
Singapore			
Manufactures[b]	94	221	24
Other	1,043	1,631	12
Total, Singapore	1,137	1,852	13

[a] Excluding canned pineapple, canned mushrooms, and canned bamboo shoots.
[b] Excluding rubber, petroleum, and road motor vehicles.
Sources:
Taiwan: Industry of Free China 38 (December 1972): 136–37.
South Korea: Monthly Economic Statistics 26 (Bank of Korea, February 1972): 77.
Singapore: Monthly Digest of Statistics 11 (Singapore: Department of Statistics, May 1972): 41–42.

items were $1,032 million, with imports from these three countries being $392 million. The other two major sources were Mexico and Hong Kong, which provided U.S. imports of $562 million.[18] These five countries accounted, therefore, for 92 percent of U.S. imports from developing countries under these two tariff items. My choice of countries was influenced by my ability to speak only English—which is spoken universally in Singapore and fairly frequently in South Korea and Taiwan—and by somewhat fortuitous contacts in Singapore, South Korea, and Taiwan.

There are no published data on the role of foreign firms in the export of manufactures from Singapore, South Korea, and Taiwan. Relying on incomplete published and unpublished material, I estimate that in 1971 foreign firms[19] accounted for at least 15

18. Data kindly made available by the U.S. Tariff Commission.
19. For the rest of this chapter, I define a foreign firm as one that is

percent of South Korea's manufactured exports, at least 20 percent of Taiwan's, and over 50 percent of Singapore's. In the last few years exports by foreign firms have probably grown more rapidly than exports by local firms in all three countries. For some products, such as television sets in Taiwan and transistors in South Korea, almost all exports are by foreign firms. For other products, such as cloth and yarn, almost all exports are by local firms.[20]

METHODOLOGY

My general initial approach for evaluating the impact of the foreign firms was to compare foreign and local firms that produce the same commodity. Except for petroleum and chemicals, every product that is a major manufactured export by foreign firms in these three countries is also produced and exported by local firms. There are eleven commodities in my sample: baseball gloves, cassettes, cloth, feed stuff, flour, radios, sewing machines, television sets, transistors, yarn, and wigs.

How did I know that the foreign firm and the local firm were in fact producing the same commodity? The answer was based mainly on my own judgment. For example, I decided that left-handed baseball gloves and right-handed baseball gloves are the same product, but I refused to compare leather baseball gloves to cotton work gloves. "Television sets" are almost all black and white portables. "Yarn" includes both synthetic yarn and cotton yarn since I was told by a plant engineer that the same machinery and workers produce both types. "Transistors" excludes integrated circuits, where the latter are distinguished both by much higher unit values and by plant managers' statements as to what they are making. "Radios" is probably the most heterogeneous commodity, ranging from pocket radios to table models, but the production techniques seem similar to me.

To preserve the confidentiality of the data, I label these prod-

---

not 100 percent owned by local citizens. For those firms in my sample having both foreign and local owners, the local share of the equity never exceeds 64 percent.

20. But see the discussion in chapter 1 concerning the definition of local firms in the textile industry.

ucts at random as A, B, C, etc. Table 3.3 shows the allocation of
the initial fifty-eight firms by product and nation. None of the
three developing countries exports all eleven commodities. Because some firms refused to participate in my study, my final

Table 3.3. Number of Firms Returning Questionnaire

	South Korea		Taiwan		Singapore		Total	
	Local	Foreign	Local	Foreign	Local	Foreign	Local	Foreign
Product								
A	2	2	1	4	1	2	4	8
B	0	0	0	3	0	0	0	3
C	1	4	1	1	0	1	2	6
D	2	0	2	0	0	1	4	1
E	4	2	1	1	1	3	6	6
F	0	0	1	1	0	0	1	1
G	0	0	0	0	1	1	1	1
H	2	1	0	1	0	0	2	2
I	0	0	0	0	1	1	1	1
J	0	0	1	2	0	0	1	2
K	1	1	1	2	0	0	2	3
Total	12	10	8	15	4	9	24	34

sample for the comparisons in the rest of this chapter is limited
to forty-six firms and nine commodities.

I chose the firms in the following way. In each of the three
countries I identified all the major foreign firms that export manufactures. I then looked for local firms making the same product.
When there were only a few local firms, I visited all of them;
when there were a great many local firms, as in textiles, I chose a
few firms on a nonrandom basis. In South Korea and Taiwan
government officials made appointments with the firms and ac-
companied me when I visited the plants. In Singapore I made
my own appointments and visited the plants alone. At each of the
eighty-five plants I explained the general purpose of my study and
my questionnaire, which is reproduced in appendix B, and toured
the plant.

Except for three companies in Singapore, every company on my
initial list agreed to see me and said they would complete the
questionnaire. Despite several follow-up letters from me in the

U.S. and follow-up telephone calls by government officials in
South Korea and Taiwan, twenty-seven firms never replied. As
shown in table 3.4, the response rate was best in South Korea,

Table 3.4. Firms Interviewed and in Sample

	Interviewed	Returned questionnaire	Percentage returning questionnaire	Number in sample
Singapore				
Local	8	4	50	4
Foreign	17	9	53	7
Total	25	13	52	11
South Korea				
Local	14	12	86	10
Foreign	11	10	91	10
Total	25	22	88	20
Taiwan				
Local	14	8	57	5
Foreign	21	15	71	10
Total	35	23	66	15
Overall				
Local	36	24	67	19
Foreign	49	34	69	27
Total	85	58	68	46

which I visited in July 1971 and in March 1972. The response
rate was lowest in Singapore, which I visited in June 1972. I was
in Taiwan in January 1973. One never gets a perfect response
rate when surveying firms, and one rarely knows if there is a
bias for those firms that do respond. There are no major differences in the response rates for foreign firms and local firms. I
would tend to view the respondent firms as a fairly complete
enumeration of the major foreign exporting firms in South Korea
and Taiwan and a somewhat random sample of the local firms
in these two countries and of all firms in Singapore.

Upon receiving each questionnaire, I checked it for internal
consistency and obvious errors. With the aid of several letters, I
was usually able to correct these problems, but I have no independent way of knowing whether firms simply gave me consistently

inaccurate information. My impression is that firms would not take the trouble to make up consistent lies; it is easier simply not to respond. It should be noted that I asked nothing about profits, taxes, or the value of capital. These are the most sensitive areas for companies. Rather than jeopardize the entire project, I asked for the type of data a plant manager could usually supply.

But even some of these data have one possible bias because of the prevalence of transfer pricing among multinational firms. Except for those local firms trying to avoid capital controls by overinvoicing imports or underinvoicing exports, the foreign trade data for local companies are based on market prices. Almost all of the exports by foreign firms are sold to the parent firm or to other subsidiaries of the same parent corporation, and many of the foreign firms' imports come from affiliated companies. The transfer prices, at least between the U.S. parent and its subsidiaries, can be arbitrarily set by the parent company provided they are "reasonably within the range of what would have been charged for similar services in an independent transaction between unrelated parties under similar circumstances." [21] One U.S. television firm in Taiwan sets its transfer price for exports on the basis of the U.S. dollar price of comparable exported Japanese television receivers. Another U.S. television firm in Taiwan sets its transfer price on a cost-plus formula. When the yen appreciated relative to the U.S. dollar, the former firm raised its transfer price and the latter did not (except to the extent that its costs rose because imports cost more). I cannot estimate either the magnitude or the direction of the bias resulting from transfer prices, since their determination involves such factors as taxes, exchange rate hedging, and negotiating strategy with governments.

As the reader will immediately notice upon looking at the tables in the remainder of this chapter, many firms that returned the questionnaire were unable, or unwilling, to complete all of it. Then why do I bother to present tables with so many cells filled in with n.a. to indicate "not available"? I do so for three reasons.

21. Decision of U.S. Court of Appeals, 29 October 1971, United States Gypsum Company v. United States of America, 452 F.2d 445 (1971), p. 447. For an economist's analysis of transfer pricing, see Jeffrey Arpan, *International Intracorporate Pricing: Non-American Systems and Views* (New York: Praeger, 1971).

First, incomplete as they are, these data represent, I believe, the largest sample for any study of foreign firms in more than one developing country, and other scholars and government officials may either find these data useful in their work or be provoked into collecting better data. Second, these incomplete data may make the reader skeptical of other studies of foreign firms, where the author presents his findings with great conviction but does not present enough of the data to allow the reader to reach his own conclusions. Finally, the alternative to presenting quantitative data taken from questionnaires is to rely on what the researcher remembers being told during a formal or informal interview. Skilled researchers have acquired valuable insights through interviews.[22] But there are dangers, especially when the researcher is publicly committed to a point of view and this point of view is shared by many of his friends and colleagues. In such a case the interviewer may only remember those parts of the interviews that are consistent with his original point of view. As the psychologist Leon Festinger put it, "Groups of scientists have been known to continue to believe in certain theories, supporting one another in this belief in spite of continual mounting evidence that these theories are incorrect." [23]

Perhaps because popular interest in foreign investment exceeds the interest of most professional economists, one or two empirical studies become the basis for broad generalizations. These generalizations are repeated until they become so widely known that scholars no longer footnote their source. This omission might not be too serious if everyone agreed, or if everyone realized there was no consensus. In fact, however, conflicting generalizations are presented by different authors, none of whom apparently realizes that others disagree.

Take, for example, the question of whether foreign manufacturing firms producing a particular product[24] adapt their technology—which was developed in rich countries with relatively ex-

22. Consider, for example, Freud's work.
23. Leon Festinger, *A Theory of Cognitive Dissonance* (Stanford, Cal.: Stanford University Press, 1957), p. 198.
24. An interesting question, which I cannot answer, is whether the mix of products exported by foreign firms is more capital-intensive than the mix of products exported by the local firms.

pensive labor and cheap capital—when they invest in developing countries with relatively cheap labor and expensive capital. As shown in supplement 2.1, the type of technology brought by foreign firms is, in theory, one of the most important variables in determining their impact on the host country. Hla Myint, in a recent study for the Asian Development Bank, says, "It is characteristic of the foreign sector, particularly in manufacturing industries, that it is not prepared to change its production method to suit local conditions." [25] Little, Scitovsky, and Scott, on the other hand, in their recent study for the OECD Development Centre, say that foreign firms "manifest greater reliance on careful calculations of costs and profitability than is customary in developing countries; and one of the outcomes of such calculation seems to be the frequent use of second-hand equipment in the plants owned and managed by foreign companies." [26] None of these eminent economists gives any evidence or citations for these statements.

The few existing empirical studies on adaptation of technology are also contradictory. Strassman, in a study of twenty-two Mexican firms and fourteen U.S. firms producing in Mexico, concluded that U.S. firms were more likely than Mexican firms to adopt labor-intensive techniques.[27] Pack, in a study of three industries in Kenya, also found that the foreign firms were more likely to use a labor-intensive technique.[28] Wells, on the other hand, using a sample of forty-three plants in six industries in Indonesia, found that foreign firms were more likely to use a capital-intensive technology.[29] Mason, in a study of fourteen U.S. firms and fourteen local firms in nine industries in Mexico and the Philippines, found that U.S. firms employed more building per worker and about the same amount of equipment per worker compared to local

25. Hla Myint, *Southeast Asia's Economy: Development Policies in the 1970's* (New York: Praeger, 1972), p. 101.
26. Little, Scitovsky, and Scott, *Industry and Trade*, p. 57.
27. W. Paul Strassman, *Technological Change and Economic Development* (Ithaca, N.Y.: Cornell University Press, 1968), pp. 190–94.
28. Howard Pack, "Employment in Kenyan Manufacturing—Some Microeconomic Evidence," mimeographed (Swarthmore, Pa., 1972).
29. He explains this result in terms of foreign firms being more likely to have monopoly profits because they make consumer products with an internationally known brand name. Louis T. Wells, Jr., "Economic Man and Engineering Man: Choice and Technology in a Low-Wage Country," *Public Policy* 21 (Summer 1973): 322.

firms.[30] Leff, in a study of twenty firms in the Brazilian capital goods industry, found that both foreign and domestic firms relied heavily on second-hand machinery imported from the rich countries.[31] Tsurumi, in a survey of forty-seven foreign manufacturing firms in Indonesia, found that foreign firms bring to Indonesia the newest equipment with which they are very familiar. This equipment is, therefore, older than the very new equipment employed by the foreign firm in its parent country (if it is still making a comparable product); the foreign firms' concern with maintenance prevents their adapting any of this familiar equipment to take advantage of Indonesian conditions.[32]

Most of the other questions about foreign investment also do not yet have agreed-upon answers. As governments obviously cannot postpone decisions on foreign investment until there is a scholarly consensus, a decision-maker should know the basis for a scholar's conclusions.

FOREIGN FIRMS AS SUPPLIERS OF CAPITAL

By comparing foreign and local firms producing and exporting the same commodity, I am assuming that local firms could expand exports if there were no foreign firms. It may be objected that local firms could not expand because of a shortage of capital. As argued, however, in chapter 2, one should in general look for the major contributions of foreign manufacturing firms in the areas of technology and management, not capital. What is true generally is also true for Taiwan, Singapore, and South Korea. The amount of capital supplied by foreign firms to these three countries is small relative to either the countries' domestic savings or alternative sources of foreign private capital.

The average Japanese or U.S. investment in South Korea has a foreign equity of only $770,000 (table 3.1). The average Japanese or U.S. project in Taiwan has a foreign equity of only $670,-

30. R. Hal Mason, "Some Observations on the Choice of Technology by Multinational Firms in Developing Countries," *Review of Economics and Statistics* 55 (August 1973): 353.

31. Nathaniel Leff, *The Brazilian Capital Goods Industry, 1929–1964* (Cambridge: Harvard University Press, 1968), pp. 26–27.

32. Yoshihiro Tsurumi, "Japanese Direct Investments in Indonesia," mimeographed (Cambridge: Harvard Business School, 1973), pp. 36–37.

000. While I do not have data on the equity of the seventeen foreign firms in my samples from Taiwan and Singapore, the ten foreign firms in my South Korean sample have an average foreign equity investment of $1,200,000.

It is true that foreign firms may contribute capital in the form of loans as well as equity. As noted earlier, loans comprise 60 percent of the foreign private capital invested in South Korea through the end of 1970. The ten foreign firms in my South Korean sample had foreign loans of $24 million. Combining the loans and equity give a total foreign capital of $36 million, or $3.6 million per foreign firm in my South Korean sample. Schreiber reports that five U.S. firms in Taiwan had a total equity of $13 million, along with $7 million borrowed in the U.S., or $4 million per firm.[33] Using an average equity and loan investment of $4 million gives $68 million for the seventeen foreign firms in my sample from Taiwan and Singapore; this estimate implies an investment of $104 million in the three countries.

Another way to estimate the capital contribution is to look at data on capital per worker. U.S. firms whose foreign subsidiaries in developing countries sold $276 million in manufactures to the U.S. in 1969 report total investment in these subsidiaries of $79 million and total employment of 66,000, or an average investment of $1,200 per employee.[34] Total employment by the twenty-seven foreign firms in my sample is about 19,000, which implies a total investment by these companies of about $23 million. This estimate may be too high, since some of the foreign companies' funds could come from local borrowing. For example, the five U.S. firms in Taiwan mentioned in the last paragraph borrowed $22 million in Taiwan, in addition to their foreign capital of $20 million.[35]

A third perspective on the capital contribution of foreign firms is to look at data on U.S. direct investment in manufacturing in all of Asia (excluding Japan), which was only $281 million during the four-year period 1969–72; of this amount, reinvested earn-

33. Jordan Schreiber, *U.S. Corporate Investment in Taiwan* (Cambridge, Mass.: University Press, 1970), p. 51.

34. U.S. Tariff Commission, *Economic Factors Affecting the Use of 807.00 and 806.30* (Washington, D.C.: U.S. Government Printing Office, 1970), pp. 152, 164.

35. Schreiber, *Corporate Investment in Taiwan*, p. 51.

ings were $181 million.[36] Profitable local firms would presumably also have reinvested. So the net contribution of new foreign capital by all U.S. manufacturing firms in all of Asia (excluding Japan) during the four years was $100 million. The U.S. firms in my sample obviously contributed only a fraction of this amount; on the other hand, there are some Japanese firms in my sample whose investments are not included in this figure.

These three alternative estimates suggest that the twenty-seven foreign firms in my sample contributed at most about $100 million in additional capital to these three countries. Is this a significant amount for these three countries? One can compare it either to their domestic savings or to alternative sources of private foreign capital.

Total domestic savings in Singapore, South Korea, and Taiwan were approximately $9.6 billion during the four years 1969–72.[37] So the capital contributed by these foreign firms to these three countries was about one percent of the countries' own savings.

A possible alternative to acquiring foreign capital through direct foreign investment is for governments of developing countries to sell bonds in world capital markets and then lend the funds to local firms. From 1969 through 1972 Singapore and South Korea sold $76 million of bonds in world capital markets. The average issue yield on bonds issued by developing countries in this period ranged from 6.5 percent to 8.9 percent.[38] While we do not have

36. Data from *Survey of Current Business,* October 1971, p. 35; *Survey of Current Business,* November 1972, pp. 29, 31; and *Survey of Current Business,* September 1973, pp. 25, 27.

37. GNP in 1970 was about $1.9 billion in Singapore, $7.9 billion in South Korea, and about $5.5 billion in Taiwan. Domestic savings in 1969 were about 15 percent of GNP in South Korea and about 18 percent of GNP in Taiwan. Lacking data on the savings rate in Singapore, I conservatively assume it is 10 percent. Applying these savings rates to these GNP data yields combined savings for the three countries of about $2.4 billion per year. GNP data for Singapore from *Finance and Development* 10 (March 1973): 27. GNP data for South Korea and Taiwan from *Trends in Developing Countries* (Washington, D.C.: International Bank for Reconstruction and Development, 1973), table 1.3. Savings rates calculated from data in *Yearbook of National Accounts Statistics 1970* (New York: United Nations, 1972).

38. Data on bond sales and interest rates from *Annual Report of the World Bank, 1972* (Washington 1972), pp. 93, 94; and *Annual Report of the World Bank, 1973* (Washington 1973), pp. 99, 100.

direct evidence on the rate of return on investments by foreign manufacturing firms in particular developing countries, the U.S. Department of Commerce estimates that between 1969 and 1971 U.S. parent firms earned 14–15 percent on their direct investment in manufacturing in all developing countries.[39]

Besides selling bonds, many developing countries can now acquire foreign capital by borrowing in the Eurocurrency market at interest rates below 14 or 15 percent. In 1972 developing countries borrowed over $3 billion in credits with maturities in excess of one year and with interest rates about 1 percent over the Eurodollar interbank rate; South Korea, for example, borrowed $30 million in Eurocurrency credits in 1972.[40]

To summarize: relative either to the countries' own savings or to their foreign private borrowings, these three developing countries have received little capital from those foreign firms concentrating on the export of manufactures.[41]

A word about the way in which the results are presented in the rest of this chapter. Readers interested in a particular question might prefer that I deal serially with each topic for all three countries. I decided, however, to present the data by country because many potential readers, and especially those in each country who helped me in this work, would prefer a coherent narrative of a particular country. The final section compares all three countries.

39. This estimate defines earnings broadly and includes branch earnings, dividends paid by the foreign subsidiary to the parent, earnings reinvested locally by the subsidiary, interest paid by the subsidiary to the parent, and royalties and fees paid by the subsidiary to the parent. *Survey of Current Business,* November 1972, p. 23.

40. This paragraph is based on a speech by Andrew Brimmer, a member of the Board of Governors of the Federal Reserve System, on 25 October 1973, and on an article in *The Economist* 249 (15 December 1973): 68–69.

41. In the case of Latin America, this is true for all investments by manufacturing firms. From 1969 through 1972 direct investment in manufacturing by all U.S. firms was $1,681 million, of which $1,060 million was reinvested earnings and $621 million was new foreign capital. During this four-year period Latin American countries raised $857 million in the international bond market and $2.3 billion in Eurocurrency credits with a maturity of more than one year. Data from same sources as cited in notes 36, 38, and 40.

SOUTH KOREA

The South Korean Foreign Capital Inducement Law says (Article 1) that foreign capital should be "conducive to the sound development of a self-sustaining national economy and to improve the international balance of payments." The Korea Trade Promotion Corporation says that this phrase implies the following priorities for foreign capital: (1) capital intensive industries, (2) industries using foreign technology, (3) industries whose exports can benefit from foreign tariff preferences, and (4) heavy chemicals.[42] The Office of Investment Promotion of the South Korean Economic Planning Board says that important considerations in approving foreign investment are the type of technology it will bring and its impact on Korea's balance of payments, existing firms in Korea, employment, and GNP.[43] These statements suggest some of the criteria one should use in looking at foreign investment.

The principal specific incentives offered by the South Korean Government for approved foreign investors are (1) complete exemption from corporate and property taxes for five years and 50 percent exemption for another three years, (2) complete exemption from customs duties for imported capital goods and for raw materials used in exports, (3) no limit on the remittance of foreign profits, and (4) no requirement on the proportion of local ownership.[44] Of 266 foreign firms licensed by the Korean government through the end of 1970, 120 are licensed solely for export and another 35 are licensed for both export and the domestic market.

As noted earlier, my sample compares ten foreign firms with ten South Korean firms that make products A, C, E, H, and K. In 1970 total South Korean exports of these five commodities were $171 million, or about 26 percent of exports of all manufactures. Plywood, clothing, and cloth are the major items—48

42. Korean Trade Promotion Corporation, *Guide for Your Investment in Korea* (Korea, n.d.), p. 24.
43. South Korea, Economic Planning Board, Office of Investment Promotion, "Foreign Direct Investment in Korea," mimeographed (n.d.), p. 4.
44. Local firms that export are also exempt from income tax and customs duties.

percent of total Korean manufactured exports—not in my sample. Refined petroleum and some chemicals are the principal manufactures exported by foreign firms that are not covered in my sample; these products accounted for about one-quarter of the 1970 exports by foreign firms. The six Japanese and four U.S. firms in my sample accounted for half of the nonpetroleum exports by foreign firms in 1970.

Of the ten foreign firms in the sample, one Japanese and three U.S. firms have no Korean equity; the remaining five Japanese firms and one U.S. firm are jointly owned with Koreans, with the Korean share of the equity ranging from 50 percent to 64 percent. Given the small size of this sample, I did not examine whether firms entirely owned by foreigners and firms owned jointly by Koreans and foreigners performed differently.

Table 3.5 shows domestic sales as a percentage of total sales. There is no consistent pattern. Sometimes all firms only export (product H); sometimes only foreign firms produce solely for export (product A); sometimes most firms produce solely for export (products C and K); and sometimes all firms export only part of their output (product E). Seven of the foreign firms and three of the local firms never sold in the domestic market; the other three foreign firms and six of the other seven local firms experienced a declining relative importance of domestic sales.

Table 3.6 shows imports for exported production as a percentage of the value of exports. Only fifteen firms supplied this information. The Korean companies import less than the foreign companies, except for the U.S. firm making product C.

Five out of seven Korean firms purchase more from other Korean firms than do foreign firms producing the same commodity (table 3.7). Of course, one cannot tell from these data the import content of these local purchases. There are no clear trends for either local purchases or imports.

The data in table 3.8—wages plus purchases in Korea (including electricity)—approximate Korean value added as a proportion of output.[45] While I did not ask for information about re-

45. I use the term "value added" in a special sense in this chapter. Since exact data are unavailable, I approximate true value added by adding wages and purchases (including electricity). This overstates actual Korean

Table 3.5. South Korea: Domestic Sales as Percentage of Total Sales

	1964	1965	1966	1967	1968	1969	1970	1971
Product A								
Korea								
1	n.a.[a]	n.a.	100	100	67	79	64	n.a.
2	—[b]	—	—	—	2	0	18	n.a.
Japan								
1	—	—	—	—	—	—	0	0
2	—	—	—	—	0	0	0	0
Product C								
Korea								
1	—	—	—	—	—	—	0	0
Japan								
1	—	—	—	—	—	—	0	0
2	—	—	—	—	—	—	0	0
U.S.								
1	—	—	—	—	0	0	0	n.a.
2	—	—	—	50	16	5	6	n.a.
Product E								
Korea								
1	100	99	95	90	90	89	68	n.a.
2	—	—	—	—	80	77	65	n.a.
3	n.a.	n.a.	n.a.	93	88	80	89	61
4	n.a.	n.a.	n.a.	n.a.	n.a.	100	95	86
Japan								
1	—	—	—	—	100	83	47	n.a.
2	95	100	100	100	100	100	72	n.a.
Product H								
Korea								
1	—	0	0	0	0	0	0	n.a.
2	n.a.	n.a.	n.a.	n.a.	0	0	0	n.a.
U.S.								
1	—	—	—	—	0	0	0	n.a.
Product K								
Korea								
1	—	3	2	1	4	3	0	n.a.
U.S.								
1	—	—	—	—	—	0	0	n.a.

[a] Not available.
[b] Firm not yet in operation.
Source: Questionnaires.

Table 3.6. South Korea: Value of Imports (excluding Tariffs and Fees) Attributed to Exports as Percentage of Value of Exports

	1964	1965	1966	1967	1968	1969	1970	1971
Product A								
Korea								
1[a]	n.a.	n.a.	n.a.	n.a.	34	56	30	n.a.
2	—	—	—	—	66	108	68	n.a.
Japan								
1	—	—	—	—	—	—	100	165
2[a]	—	—	—	—	100	89	70	44
Product C								
Korea								
1	—	—	—	—	—	—	59	47
Japan								
1[a]	—	—	—	—	—	—	88	98
2[a]	—	—	—	—	—	—	43	n.a.
U.S.								
1	—	—	—	—	n.a.	n.a.	n.a.	n.a.
2	—	—	—	58	22	31	35	n.a.
Product E								
Korea								
1	n.a.	n.a.	n.a.	n.a.	n.a.	n.a.	n.a.	n.a.
2	—	—	—	—	n.a.	n.a.	n.a.	n.a.
3	n.a.	n.a.	n.a.	59	62	61	74	89
4	n.a.	n.a.	n.a.	n.a.	n.a.	n.a.	17	16
Japan								
1[a]	—	—	—	—	—	66	105	n.a.
2	n.a.	n.a.	n.a.	n.a.	n.a.	n.a.	n.a.	n.a.
Product H								
Korea								
1	—	n.a.	n.a.	n.a.	30	30	24	n.a.
2	n.a.	n.a.	n.a.	n.a.	30	28	26	n.a.
U.S.								
1	—	—	—	—	28	41	44	n.a.
Product K								
Korea								
1	—	n.a.	n.a.	n.a.	n.a.	n.a.	n.a.	n.a.
U.S.								
1	—	—	—	—	—	8	64	n.a.

[a] Imports include tariffs and other fees.
Note: The proportion of total imports attributed to exports is assumed equal to the proportion of total sales that is exported.
Source: Questionnaires.

Table 3.7. South Korea: Purchases from Korean Firms (excluding Electricity) as Percentage of Value of Output

	1964	1965	1966	1967	1968	1969	1970	1971
Product A								
Korea								
1	n.a.	n.a.	n.a.	n.a.	38	33	32	n.a.
2	—	—	—	—	4	3	28	n.a.
Japan								
1	—	—	—	—	—	—	1	1
2	—	—	—	—	0	11	30	56
Product C								
Korea								
1	—	—	—	—	—	—	8	9
Japan								
1	—	—	—	—	—	—	1	1
2	—	—	—	—	—	—	n.a.	n.a.
U.S.								
1	—	—	—	—	n.a.	n.a.	n.a.	n.a.
2	—	—	—	4	3	1	2	n.a.
Product E								
Korea								
1	n.a.	n.a.	n.a.	n.a.	n.a.	n.a.	n.a.	n.a.
2	—	—	—	—	n.a.	n.a.	n.a.	n.a.
3	n.a.	n.a.	n.a.	9	8	7	5	6
4	n.a.	n.a.	n.a.	n.a.	n.a.	4	4	4
Japan								
1	—	—	—	—	1	1	1	n.a.
2	n.a.	n.a.	n.a.	n.a.	n.a.	n.a.	n.a.	n.a.
Product H								
Korea								
1	—	n.a.	n.a.	n.a.	7	2	10	n.a.
2	n.a.	n.a.	n.a.	n.a.	51	28	21	n.a.
U.S.								
1	—	—	—	—	40	18	13	n.a.
Product K								
Korea								
1	—	n.a.	n.a.	n.a.	n.a.	n.a.	n.a.	n.a.
U.S.								
1	—	—	—	—	—	0	0	n.a.

Source: Questionnaires.

Table 3.8. South Korea: Wages plus Local Purchases (including
Electricity) as Percentage of Value of Output

	1964	1965	1966	1967	1968	1969	1970	1971
Product A								
Korea								
1	n.a.	n.a.	n.a.	n.a.	40	35	36	n.a.
2[a]	—	—	—	—	10	9	38	n.a.
Japan								
1	—	—	—	—	—	—	12	17
2	—	—	—	—	8	17	37	65
Product C								
Korea								
1	—	—	—	—	—	—	17	20
Japan								
1	—	—	—	—	—	—	9	9
2	—	—	—	—	—	—	n.a.	n.a.
U.S.								
1	—	—	—	—	n.a.	n.a.	n.a.	n.a.
2	—	—	—	11	25	30	36	n.a.
Product E								
Korea								
1	n.a.	n.a.	n.a.	n.a.	n.a.	n.a.	n.a.	n.a.
2	—	—	—	—	n.a.	n.a.	n.a.	n.a.
3	n.a.	n.a.	n.a.	n.a.	n.a.	19	18	14
4	n.a.	n.a.	n.a.	n.a.	n.a.	n.a.	n.a.	n.a.
Japan								
1	—	—	—	—	11	11	9	n.a.
2	n.a.	n.a.	n.a.	n.a.	n.a.	n.a.	n.a.	n.a.
Product H								
Korea								
1	—	n.a.	n.a.	n.a.	n.a.	n.a.	28	n.a.
2	n.a.	n.a.	n.a.	n.a.	n.a.	46	43	n.a.
U.S.								
1	—	—	—	—	58	37	34	n.a.
Product K								
Korea								
1	—	n.a.	n.a.	n.a.	n.a.	n.a.	n.a.	n.a.
U.S.								
1	—	—	—	—	—	9	8	n.a.

[a] Excludes electricity.
Source: Questionnaires.

invested profits, my impression is that foreign companies in all
three countries tend to repatriate all their earnings and that local
companies reinvest a large portion, frequently in other local
industries. For example, a large South Korean firm making consumer electrical goods (like fans and radios) mainly for local
markets invested in the first local transistor company; a large
Taiwanese firm exporting yarn and cloth has sister companies
that are engaged in producing cement, running department stores,
making garments, and trucking; this firm also established a technical institute. I found no examples of foreign firms reinvesting
their profits in other local industries. A reader who is surprised
at this pattern should speculate on what U.S. economic history
would have been like if such families as the DuPonts, Rockefellers,
and Mellons had lived in Europe.

Some readers may be surprised at how little value added the
Korean and foreign firms yield. In 1970 only one company had
value added in excess of 40 percent of the value of output, and
six of the thirteen companies had value added of less than 20
percent of the value of output.[46] For product E the Korean firm
shows a higher proportion of value added than does the foreign
firm; for product C the Korean company is between the two foreign companies; for product H, the foreign company is between the
two Korean companies; for product A one foreign firm has less
value added and one about the same as the two Korean firms.

One might object that this comparison of the value added of
different firms is unnecessary on the grounds that the alternative
to a Korean's working for a foreign firm is to be unemployed.

value added to the extent that items purchased from Korean firms contain
imported components. On the other hand, this tends to understate Korean
value added by excluding the annual contribution of land and the depreciation of buildings and of Korean machinery used in the production
of these commodities.

46. By comparison, U.S. manufacturing firms in Latin America have
payments for wages and for local materials, supplies, and services equal to
about 68 percent of sales, with wages accounting for about 18 percent of
sales. Vernon, *Sovereignty at Bay,* p. 101. Most of these companies produce
for the local market. Arthur Lewis observes that wages and salaries as a
share of value added in manufacturing are much lower in developing countries (about 20 to 30 percent) than in rich countries (40 to 60 percent).
W. Arthur Lewis, *Aspects of Tropical Trade 1883–1965* (Stockholm:
Almqvist and Wiksell, 1969), pp. 32–33.

There apparently is no consensus among observers of the Korean economy as to whether substantial unemployment—open or disguised—exists.[47] The open unemployment rate fell steadily from 7.4 percent in 1965 to 4.5 percent in 1970. Those employed less than eighteen hours per week fell from 7.3 percent of the labor force in 1965 to 4.7 percent in 1970. The proportion of the population aged fourteen and over that was in the labor force rose from 55 percent in 1965–67 to 56 percent in 1968–70. Employment in manufacturing rose by 57.5 percent between 1967 and 1970. Real wages for both industrial and rural workers increased steadily after 1964.[48] Money wages in most firms rose by more than the 15 percent increase in the urban cost-of-living index between 1969 and 1970 (table 3.9). I conclude from all these data that by 1970 there was little unemployment in the Korean economy.[49] Even if there were unemployed labor, an alternative to direct foreign investment would be expansion of Korean firms financed by foreign borrowing.

For most products there is no clear wage pattern between foreign firms and Korean firms in 1970. It should be noted that this interpretation of the average annual wage per worker assumes that each firm has the same mixture of skill levels in its labor

47. For example, Gustav Ranis said in 1971 that "it is still somewhat doubtful that recent wage increases really signal the end of Korea's labor surplus condition." Gustav Ranis, "The Role of the Industrial Sector in Korea's Transition to Economic Maturity," in *Basic Documents and Selected Papers of Korea's Third Five-Year Economic Development Plan (1972–1976)*, ed. Sung Hwan Jo and Seong-Yawng Park (Seoul, 1972), p. 47.

48. This analysis relies heavily on a paper by Roger Sedjo, "The Turning Point for the Korean Economy," in Jo and Park, eds., *Basic Documents and Selected Papers*, pp. 207–21. It would be helpful to have data on changes in real wages for unskilled workers, since part of the observed increase in real wages represents changes in the skill composition of the labor force and in the relative wages of different types of workers. For example, in Colombia between 1958 and 1964 real wages in large manufacturing firms (the modern ones) rose by 37 percent while real wages in very small manufacturing firms (the craft ones) fell by 10 percent. Richard R. Nelson, T. Paul Schultz, and Robert L. Slighton, *Structural Change in a Developing Economy: Colombia's Problems and Prospects* (Princeton: Princeton University Press, 1971), pp. 136–38.

49. This conclusion assumes no change in production technology and no change in consumption patterns, including the way retail trade and urban services are organized.

Table 3.9. South Korea: Average Annual Wages (Thousand won)

	Male 1969	Male 1970	Female 1969	Female 1970	Percentage change Male	Percentage change Female
Product A						
Korea						
1	200	292	110	120	46	9
2	346	288	83	122	−17	46
Japan						
1	—	442[a]	—	110[a]	—	—
2	114	120	102	108	5	6
Product C						
Korea						
1	—	145[a]	—	80[a]	—	—
Japan						
1	—	330[a]	—	75[a]	—	—
2	—	321[a]	—	117[a]	—	—
U.S.						
1	n.a.	n.a.	n.a.	n.a.	—	—
2	453	458	132	164	1	24
Product E						
Korea						
1	n.a.	n.a.	n.a.	n.a.	—	—
2	292	324	107	124	11	16
3	195	193	114	116	−1	2
4	n.a.	n.a.	n.a.	n.a.	—	—
Japan						
1	288	347	126	124	20	−2
2	154	248	60	76	61	27
Product H						
Korea						
1	n.a.	464	n.a.	95	—	—
2	n.a.	446	n.a.	136	—	—
U.S.						
1	235	325	76	118	38	55
Product K						
Korea						
1	144	170	116	137	18	18
U.S.						
1	96[a]	120	72[a]	96	25	33

[a] Based on partial year response.
Source: Questionnaires.

force. It is possible, for example, that foreign firms pay their highly skilled workers more than Korean firms and have fewer highly skilled workers than Korean firms, so that both types of firms have the same average wage. The skill mix for female workers, however, is probably roughly the same for all firms. While the average annual male wage in 1970 ranged from W120,000 to W464,000, the average annual female wage in 1970 ranged from W75,000 to W137,000, and eleven of the seventeen companies had an average annual female wage between W95,000 and W125,000. Even for females there is no pattern in 1970. For products A and K the Korean firms pay more than the foreign firms. For product E, one foreign firm pays more and the other less than the two Korean firms. For product C two foreign firms pay more and one foreign firm pays less than the local firm. For product H the foreign firm's wage is between that of the two local firms. It should be noted that my wage data exclude the value of dormitory facilities and other fringe benefits, which differ among firms. My impression is that geography is the main determinant of whether a firm has dormitories. In Seoul no firm does; in smaller towns almost every firm does.

To what extent do foreign firms serve as a school, training Koreans who then work for Korean firms? First, it should be observed that most Koreans have never worked for any company other than their current employer; this is especially true for assembly line workers, most of whom are women who have come directly from farms to work in factories. A sample of thirty-six female workers, arbitrarily selected by me during tours of twenty-one factories, revealed that 52 percent of those working in Seoul had fathers who were farmers and 85 percent of those working in other cities (Anyang, Suwon, and Pusan) had fathers who were farmers.[50] Table 3.10 indicates that for only two firms—both foreign—

50. This is not a universal pattern in developing countries. For example, in Colombia, where literacy is much lower than in Korea, female migrants from rural areas apparently go into the urban service sector rather than directly into manufacturing. Nelson, Schultz, and Slighton, *Structural Change*, pp. 53, 57, 149–52. On the other hand, Puerto Rico in the early 1950s seems to resemble Korea. Over two-thirds of female factory workers lived in rural areas prior to employment, and only 45 percent of the women had had a job before working in a factory, as compared with 78

Table 3.10. South Korea: Previous Employment, by Number of Firms

	Firms answering	Workers previously employed			
		More than 50%	31–50%	11–30%	10% or less
Assembly					
Men					
Korean	8	1	0	1	6
Foreign	10	4	0	3	3
Women					
Korean	8	0	1	1	6
Foreign	10	2	2	1	5
Supervisory					
Korean	8	2	0	3	3
Foreign	10	4	0	0	6

Source: Questionnaires.

had at least half the female labor force been previously employed by other firms. About half the firms reported that less than 10 percent of their employees (assembly line and supervisory) had been previously employed.[51] While foreign firms seem more likely than Korean firms to hire assembly line workers with previous employment experience, there is no pattern on supervisory personnel.

Of those workers previously employed, only one Korean firm reported that more than 30 percent had worked for foreign firms (table 3.11); this Korean firm is in the only industry where foreigners were the first producers. Almost all the other Korean firms and most of the foreign firms reported that none of their workers had previously worked for a foreign firm.

---

percent of the men. Lloyd Reynolds and Peter Gregory, *Wages, Productivity, and Industrialization in Puerto Rico* (Homewood, Ill.: Richard D. Irwin, 1965), pp. 207–09.

51. Comparable data for other countries are scarce. A study of the U.S. labor force found that 11 percent of all males and 9 percent of all females held at least two jobs during 1961; presumably a larger percentage have had at least two jobs sometime during their lives. Turnover is much higher for younger workers in the U.S. For those under 25, 19 percent of males and 15 percent of females had held at least two jobs during 1961. Most of the workers in my survey, especially the females, seemed to be under twenty-five. U.S. data from Gertrude Bancroft and Stuart Garfinkle, "Job Mobility in 1961," *Monthly Labor Review* 86 (August 1963): 898.

Table 3.11. South Korea: Workers Previously Employed by Foreign
Firms as Percentage of All Those Previously Employed

	Firms answering	More than 50%	31–50%	11–30%	1–10%	0%
Korean firms	6	0	1	1	0	4
Foreign firms	8	0	0	1	2	5

Source: Questionnaires.

This relatively low labor turnover may be due both to workers' attitudes toward the propriety of changing jobs and to firms' wage policies. If workers (and managers) learn over time as a natural part of the production process, then a firm which seeks to maximize profits will pay a wage above the prevailing market wage in order to reduce the number of workers who quit. If workers (and managers) learn separately from the production process (by, say, being sent to a special technical school), then a firm will also raise wages above the prevailing market rate for those workers who have learned skills useful only in that firm (e.g., the firm's procedures for keeping records). The firm will not, however, raise wages—and may even lower them during the training period—for workers whose skills (such as typing) can be used elsewhere.[52]

As for managerial personnel, my impression from my interviews is that few managers in Korean firms had worked for foreign firms; the military seems to be the principal training ground for managers and technicians.[53]

Output per worker differs greatly among firms producing the same product. To what extent can these differences be explained by differences in capital, in economies of scale, and in learning?

Much of the machinery used by foreign firms in Korea was used elsewhere before being brought to Korea. Its value on the

52. For the assumptions and theoretical arguments to support these assertions, see Gary S. Becker, "Investment in On-the-Job Training," and Richard S. Eckaus, "Comment on Becker's Analysis of On-the-Job Training," both in *Economics of Education*, vol. 1, ed. M. Blaug (Baltimore: Penguin Books, 1968).

53. Again, this seems different from Colombia, where apparently "many Colombian businessmen have served their managerial apprenticeships in foreign firms." Nelson, Schultz, and Slighton, *Structural Change*, p. 283.

books of the firm in Korea is heavily influenced by the tax laws of Korea and of the country of the parent firm. In order to compare mechanization among firms, I therefore ignore financial data on capital stock and use electricity consumption, on the assumption that for a particular commodity the technologies are sufficiently similar that the extent of mechanization is proportional to electricity consumption.[54] This approach also voids the problem of different utilization rates. If one compares capital/labor ratios using the value of capital, differences in the ratios can be due either to differences in the type of capital or to differences in utilization rates. My impression, based on interviews with plant managers, is that utilization rates for the same product do not differ between foreign and local firms.

The evidence is mixed as to whether small firms in Korea use more labor-intensive techniques than large firms. Table 3.12 shows that a Korean firm has the largest output for three of the five products. Table 3.13 shows electricity consumption per worker. The rank correlations between electricity per worker and level of output in 1970 are: zero for product C (five firms); −1.0 for product A (two firms); 1.0 for products K (two firms) and H (three firms); and .3 for product E (five firms).

The evidence is also mixed as to whether foreign firms are less mechanized. For two products (H and K) the foreign firms are less mechanized than the Korean firms. For product C in 1970 the two Japanese companies and one U.S. company have less capital per worker than the Korean company; the other U.S. company has more capital per worker than the Korean or Japanese companies. For product E two Korean firms are between the two Japanese firms, and one Korean firm has much less capital per worker. This ranking by electricity consumption agrees with my subjective rankings of relative mechanization formed during my tours of the plants (before seeing the data on electricity consumption). As for trends in mechanization, only three firms supplied data for at least four years. Two show no trend, and one shows a steady increase in mechanization. Rising money wages have been

54. This approach also assumes that all firms have the same proportion of machinery and buildings, so that total capital can be compared by looking at machinery alone.

Table 3.12. South Korea: Average Monthly Output in 1970

	Per worker	Total
Product A		
Korea		
1	67	13,477
2	16	1,733
Japan		
1	45	6,088
2	58	20,141
Product C		
Korea		
1	6,214	447,417
Japan		
1	8,777	658,333
2	9,385	3,031,583
U.S.		
1	9,838	21,603,750
2	5,516	11,920,500
Product E		
Korea		
1	2,012	2,337,632
2	711	1,101,112
3	1,140	1,269,478
4	511	435,023
Japan		
1	1,977	261,021
2	695	1,604,583
Product H		
Korea		
1	81	62,998
2	95	446,735
U.S.		
1	65	57,867
Product K		
Korea		
1	213	36,712
U.S.		
1	133	16,000

Source: Questionnaires.

Table 3.13. South Korea: Annual Electricity Consumption per Worker (Kilowatt-hours)

	1964	1965	1966	1967	1968	1969	1970	1971
Product A								
Korea								
1	n.a.	n.a.	n.a.	n.a.	n.a.	n.a.	n.a.	n.a.
2	—	—	—	—	n.a.	n.a.	n.a.	n.a.
Japan								
1	—	—	—	—	—	—	670[a]	585[a]
2	—	—	—	—	240	198	210	218
Product C								
Korea								
1	—	—	—	—	—	—	2,736	1,339
Japan								
1	—	—	—	—	—	—	2,053[a]	3,700[a]
2	—	—	—	—	—	—	2,463[a]	n.a.
U.S.								
1	—	—	—	—	4,243	2,964	3,480	n.a.
2	—	—	—	n.a.	n.a.	996	1,265	n.a.
Product E								
Korea								
1	n.a.	n.a.	n.a.	n.a.	n.a.	n.a.	n.a.	n.a.
2	—	—	—	—	n.a.	10,314	11,291	n.a.
3	n.a.	n.a.	n,a.	n.a.	n.a.	6,585	16,052	20,367
4	n.a.	n.a.	n.a.	n.a.	n.a.	3,143	4,845	9,810
Japan								
1	—	—	—	—	11,826[a]	16,644	18,098	n.a.
2	13,087	16,060	11,801	8,749	6,777	9,224	10,059	n.a.
Product H								
Korea								
1	—	n.a.	n.a.	n.a.	n.a.	n.a.	155	n.a.
2	n.a.	n.a.	n.a.	n.a.	n.a.	n.a.	554	n.a.
U.S.								
1	—	—	—	—	130	119	153	n.a.
Product K								
Korea								
1	—	1,102	1,022	1,255	1,530	1,728	2,410	n.a.
U.S.								
1	—	—	—	—	—	393	242	n.a.

[a] Based on partial year response.

Source: Questionnaires.

at least partially offset for exporters by a gradual depreciation of the exchange rate, which was W270 per U.S. dollar in 1966 and W373 per U.S. dollar in 1971.

The data indicate, as one might expect, that output per worker is positively related to electricity consumption per worker. One gets a hint that other things besides capital per worker influence output per worker by examining product C, where the two Japanese producers have output per worker about 50 percent greater than the Korean company even though their consumption of electricity per worker is less.

Economies of scale and learning are two elements that could affect output per worker. Monthly output levels fluctuate greatly for these firms. Even looking only at the last six months of the period, when most firms had been operating for many months, one finds the ratio of maximum monthly output to minimum monthly output (table 3.14) to be at least 1.4 for six of the nine companies for which I could obtain monthly production data. If there were short-run economies of scale or if the level of employment were fixed in the short run, then the monthly output level would influence monthly output per worker.

When a firm begins operations, output per worker is low; as workers and managers gain experience, output per worker gradually rises even with no new investment. Reynolds and Gregory, for example, studied Puerto Rico in the early 1950s, and found "many instances of plants which had managed to double physical product per employee within a few years and with little increase in the amount of capital employed." [55]

We do not have an empirically verified theory for explaining learning, whether it is of reading by children[56] or of production by workers.[57] Economists examining labor productivity have sug-

55. Reynolds and Gregory, *Industrialization in Puerto Rico,* p. 295.

56. See U.S. Office of Education, *Equality of Educational Opportunity* (Washington, D.C.: U.S. Government Printing Office, 1966); and S. Bowles and H. Levin, "The Determinants of Scholastic Achievements: An Appraisal of Some Recent Evidence," *Journal of Human Resources* (Winter 1968), pp. 3–24.

57. See Ivar Berg, *Education and Jobs: The Great Training Robbery* (Boston: Beacon Press, 1971).

Table 3.14. South Korea: Ratio of Maximum Monthly Output to
Minimum Monthly Output, Last Six Months of Sample Period

Product A	
Japan	
1	5.5
2	1.9
Product C	
Korea	
1	1.5
Japan	
1	7.2
2	1.2
U.S.	
2	1.6
Product E	
Japan	
1	1.3
Product H	
U.S.	
1	1.5
Product K	
U.S.	
1	1.1

Source: Questionnaires.

gested three explanatory variables for learning: the passage of time, cumulative output, and investment.[58]

With no firmly based theory as to what are the key explanatory variables, it is not surprising that the functional form cannot always be predicted a priori.[59] One possibility is that learning reaches a maximum level and looks like the logistic curve in diagram 3.1 (which uses cumulative output for reasons given in supplement 3.1). The econometric analysis in supplement 3.1

58. Kenneth J. Arrow, "The Economic Implications of Learning by Doing," *Review of Economic Studies* 29 (June 1962): 155–73.
59. Psychologists have found that "for perceptual-motor skills, the attainment of an asymptote or limit of skill with long-continued practice is more an exception than the rule." James Deese and Steward Hulse, *The Psychology of Learning,* 3rd ed. (New York: McGraw-Hill Book Co., 1967), p. 453.

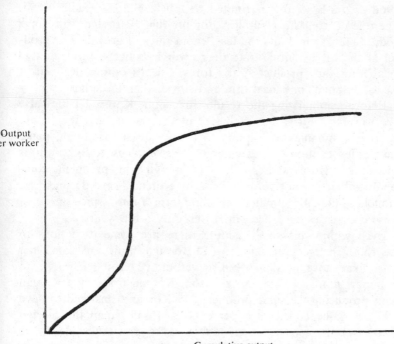

Cumulative output

Diagram 3.1. Learning Curve for a Firm

suggests that in general the logistic curve gives a satisfactory explanation of learning for seven of the nine firms supplying monthly data on employment and output. These results do not, of course, tell us who is learning. Is it management, workers, or suppliers? Does learning to produce more physical units per worker also lead to producing more cheaply? While these firms seem now to be on a plateau of monthly output per worker, will they subsequently move to a higher plateau? What happens to learning as new models are introduced? As many of these firms have been operating less than two years, it would be interesting to examine their performance again to try to answer some of these questions.

Finally, which firms have grown most rapidly? Even when using

1968 as the base, one is limited to fourteen firms (table 3.15). There is no consistent pattern. For product E foreign firms have both the most rapid and the least rapid rates of growth. For product H the foreign firm's rate of growth is between those of two local firms. For product A the foreign firm's output declined at the same rate as one local firm and slower than the other.

Before summarizing the results for South Korea, let me raise two warnings. First, the small size of the sample and the failure of some companies to respond to all my questions should make the reader cautious in extending these findings to other firms operating in Korea and especially to foreign firms producing commodities that are not yet produced by Korean firms. Second, one cannot confidently predict the long-term future since most of these companies have been in Korea only a few years.

Even within this small sample there are some exceptions to the following generalizations: (1) foreign firms are somewhat more likely to export their entire output; (2) foreign firms tend to import more and to buy less from Korean firms than Korean firms producing the same product; (3) Korean firms tend to have a higher value added as a percentage of sales than the foreign firms; (4) there is no clear pattern as to pay scales, levels of mechanization, and relative size between foreign and Korean firms; (5) there is no clear trend toward increasing mechanization; (6) very few Koreans who work for a Korean company have been previously employed by a foreign firm; and (7) learning seems to be a significant factor in explaining output per worker.

SINGAPORE

Singapore had a small manufacturing sector in the 1950s. In 1959 there were 534 establishments employing at least ten workers, with total output of $S399 million and total value added of $S143 million.[60] In 1959 legislation was passed which gave approved firms "Pioneer" status; the main advantages of such status

---

60. These data exclude firms engaged in rubber processing.

Table 3.15. South Korea: Annual Percentage
Rate of Growth of Output, 1968–70

Product A
Korea
  1   −16
  2   −39
Japan
  1   —[a]
  2   −15

Product C
Korea
  1   —
Japan
  1   —
  2   —
U.S.
  1   72
  2   60

Product E
Korea
  1   9
  2   20
  3   12
  4   n.a.
Japan
  1   40
  2   6

Product H
Korea
  1   32
  2   135
U.S.
  1   90

Product K
Korea
  1   77
U.S.
  1   —

[a] Not applicable: no output in 1968.
Source: Questionnaires.

were exemption from corporate income tax for five years, acceler-
ated depreciation, and exemption from import duties on raw
materials and equipment. Existing firms were given more limited
concessions if they expanded capacity. By 1966 111 Pioneer firms
were in production; they accounted for 20 percent of all employment in manufacturing and brought Singapore such new products
as cement, paint, flour, and textiles.[61] Value added of all manufacturing firms almost tripled, rising to $S415 million by 1966.

As mentioned earlier, there were only sixteen foreign manufacturing firms in Singapore in 1959; by 1966, 136 had been approved (out of a total of over 1,100 firms employing at least ten
workers). A majority of these foreign firms invested in Singapore
in order to serve the local market, which, in the first half of the
1960s, included all of the Malaysian Federation. Many overseas
Chinese invested in Singapore because it was culturally familiar
and seemed politically secure.[62]

In the late 1960s several large U.S. and European companies
set up factories whose entire output is exported. Most of these
companies were unwilling to return my questionnaire. A U.S.
firm making product C did return the questionnaire, but there are
no local firms making product C. A Japanese-Hong Kong company making product D is also excluded because there is no local
firm making product D. So in this section I am limited to comparing seven foreign companies and four local companies making
products A, E, G, and I. Two of these foreign companies have
capital from both Hong Kong and Japan; the others have their
entire foreign capital from Hong Kong. I could obtain data on
the proportion of local ownership for only four of the seven foreign companies; two of them have no local equity and the other
two have 50 percent local equity. As about 75 percent of Singapore's population is Chinese, one should bear in mind that firms
owned by overseas Chinese are frequently linked to Singaporeans
by marriage as well as equity.

Only the two firms making product I were operating before

61. This paragraph is based on the excellent description of Singapore
in chapters 1 and 8 of *Industrialisation in Singapore,* ed. Hughes and You.
62. This summary of the motives for foreign invtstment in Singapore
through 1966 is based on chapter 8 of ibid.

1967 (table 3.16). While the local firm making product I relied more heavily on the local market at the end of the period, exports became relatively more important for the foreign firm, at least through 1968. For the other nine firms, making products A,

Table 3.16. Singapore: Domestic Sales as Percentage of Total Sales

	1964	1965	1966	1967	1968	1969	1970	1971
Product A								
Singapore								
1	—	—	—	—	—	—	—	0
Hong Kong								
1	—	—	—	—	—	0	8	8
2	—	—	—	—	—	0	0	0
Product E								
Singapore								
1	—	—	—	—	—	—	—	5
Japan and								
Hong Kong								
1	—	—	—	—	—	—	7	10
2	—	—	—	—	—	43	43	43
Hong Kong								
1	—	—	—	—	—	—	56	47
Product G								
Singapore								
1	—	—	—	—	—	—	79	60
Hong Kong								
1	—	—	—	65	65	65	65	65
Product I								
Singapore								
1	49	37	65	53	63	69	75	74
Hong Kong								
1	71	65	56	47	44	46	48	56

Source: Questionnaires.

E, and G, there is not much trend in the relative importance of exports. The local firms export relatively more than the foreign firms for products E and G and more than one foreign firm for product A.

The propensity to import can only be compared for product G, where both the foreign firm and the local firm import about the same amount (table 3.17). Local firms and foreign firms buy about the same amount from local firms for products E and G, but for product A the local firm buys considerably more from local firms than does either of the two foreign firms (table 3.18).

As shown in table 3.19, value added—wages plus local purchases—is higher for the foreign firm making product G and for one foreign firm making product E. The local firm has a higher value added for product A. As in the case of South Korea, many

Table 3.17. Singapore: Value of Imports (excluding Tariffs and Fees) Attributed to Exports as Percentage of Value of Exports

	1964	1965	1966	1967	1968	1969	1970	1971
Product A								
Singapore								
1	—	—	—	—	—	—	—	n.a.
Hong Kong								
1	—	—	—	—	—	172	119	84
2	—	—	—	—	—	116	65	n.a.
Product E								
Singapore								
1	—\	—	—	—	—	—	—	n.a.
Japan and								
Hong Kong								
1	—	—	—	—	—	—	185	92
2	—	—	—	—	—	n.a.	n.a.	n.a.
Hong Kong								
1	—	—	—	—	—	—	41	40
Product G								
Singapore								
1[a]	—	—	—	—	—	—	79	83
Hong Kong								
1	—	—	—	83	82	82	87	85
Product I								
Singapore								
1	n.a.	n.a.	n.a.	n.a.	n.a.	n.a.	n.a.	n.a.
Hong Kong								
1	108	96	86	83	86	75	87	68

[a] Imports include fees.

Note: The proportion of total imports attributed to exports is assumed equal to the proportion of total sales that is exported.

Source: Questionnaires.

Table 3.18. Singapore: Purchases from Singaporean Firms
(excluding Electricity) as Percentage of Value of Output

	1964	1965	1966	1967	1968	1969	1970	1971
Product A								
Singapore								
1	—	—	—	—	—	—	—	82
Hong Kong								
1	—	—	—	—	—	n.a.	15	13
2	—	—	—	—	—	16	31	n.a.
Product E								
Singapore								
1	—	—	—	—	—	—	—	2
Japan and								
Hong Kong								
1	—	—	—	—	—	—	1	1
2	—	—	—	—	—	n.a.	n.a.	n.a.
Hong Kong								
1	—	—	—	—	—	—	3	3
Product G								
Singapore								
1	—	—	—	—	—	—	0	0
Hong Kong								
1	—	—	—	2	3	2	2	2
Product I								
Singapore								
1	n.a.	n.a.	n.a.	n.a.	n.a.	n.a.	n.a.	n.a.
Hong Kong								
1	6	5	6	7	5	4	6	5

Source: Questionnaires.

firms have a value added of less than 20 percent of the value of output. But in Singapore 44 percent of the firms in the sample have value added in excess of 40 percent of output, compared to only 7 percent of the South Korean firms.

Since only one local company reported electricity consumption, a comparison is limited to product I (table 3.20). The local firm is more mechanized than the foreign firm. Looking at trends, all five foreign firms are becoming increasingly mechanized, while the one local firm reporting remains at roughly the same level of mechanization.

Table 3.19. Singapore: Wages plus Local Purchases (including
Electricity) as Percentage of Value of Output

	1964	1965	1966	1967	1968	1969	1970	1971
Product A								
Singapore								
1[a]	—	—	—	—	—	—	—	97
Hong Kong								
1	—	—	—	—	—	n.a.	59	44
2	—	—	—	—	—	43	50	n.a.
Product E								
Singapore								
1	—	—	—	—	—	—	—	16
Japan and								
Hong Kong								
1	—	—	—	—	—	—	16	16
2	—	—	—	—	—	n.a.	n.a.	n.a.
Hong Kong								
1	—	—	—	—	—	—	40	43
Product G								
Singapore								
1	—	—	—	—	—	—	2	2
Hong Kong								
1	—	—	—	9	6	6	6	6
Product I								
Singapore								
1	n.a.	n.a.	n.a.	n.a.	n.a.	n.a.	n.a.	n.a.
Hong Kong								
1	12	9	9	10	8	8	10	10

ᵃ Excludes electricity.
Source: Questionnaires.

My own impressions of several large foreign plants will supplement the statistical data on mechanization. Since these companies
did not return my questionnaire, I will name them. General Electric has a large factory making radios. It appeared very automated, and I was told that the techniques were the same as in
the U.S. Philips also has a large radio factory. Its techniques are
more labor intensive than those of General Electric, and Philips
has its own designers and machine shops for adapting foreign machinery. In the summer of 1972, General Electric was running

Table 3.20. Singapore: Annual Electricity Consumption per Worker
(Kilowatt-hours)

	1964	1965	1966	1967	1968	1969	1970	1971
Product A								
Singapore								
1	—	—	—	—	—	—	—	n.a.
Hong Kong								
1	—	—	—	—	—	184	472	682
2	—	—	—	—	—	n.a.	n.a.	n.a.
Product E								
Singapore								
1	—	—	—	—	—	—	—	n.a.
Japan and								
Hong Kong								
1	—	—	—	—	—	—	11,330ᵃ	15,348
2	—	—	—	—	—	n.a.	n.a.	n.a.
Hong Kong								
1	—	—	—	—	—	—	13,562	18,348
Product G								
Singapore								
1	—	—	—	—	—	—	n.a.	n.a.
Hong Kong								
1	—	—	—	5,167	8,500	9,493	11,500	14,250
Product I								
Singapore								
1	57,372	49,904	57,041	67,055	57,308	64,996	48,936	42,802
Hong Kong								
1	14,902	17,751	27,993	32,533	37,188	29,195	28,751	29,233

ᵃ Based on partial year response.
Source: Questionnaires.

two shifts and Philips one shift. Both General Electric and Philips
seem to me to be more capital-intensive than local firms making
radios. National Semiconductor and Texas Instruments both
make integrated circuits in large factories; both factories are very
automated, use new machinery imported from the U.S., and run
three shifts. There are no local firms making products as sophisticated as those of National Semiconductor and Texas Instruments.
My impression—that three out of four large foreign companies
are using very automated production techniques in Singapore—is

Table 3.21. Singapore: Average Annual Wages
(Singapore dollars)

	Male		Female		Percentage change	
	1970	1971	1970	1971	Male	Female
Product A						
Singapore						
1	—	3,820[a]	—	1,240[a]	—	—
Hong Kong						
1	n.a.	n.a.	n.a.	n.a.	n.a.	n.a.
2	n.a.	n.a.	n.a.	n.a.	n.a.	n.a.
Product E						
Singapore						
1	—	4,000[a]	—	2,790[a]	—	—
Japan and						
Hong Kong						
1	1,810[a]	2,440	1,800[a]	2,440	35	36
2	3,290	4,060	1,430	1,740	23	22
Hong Kong						
1	3,760	4,900	1,230	1,790	30	46
Product G						
Singapore						
1	n.a.	n.a.	n.a.	n.a.	n.a.	n.a.
Hong Kong						
1	21,670[b]	23,330[b]	3,430	3,570	8	4
Product I						
Singapore						
1	n.a.	n.a.	n.a.	n.a.	n.a.	n.a.
Hong Kong						
1	4,560	5,190	4,040	4,700	14	16

[a] Based on partial year response.
[b] Including management.
Source: Questionnaires.

consistent with the conclusion of Hughes and You, who studied
119 firms from six countries in the mid-1960s; they found that
"there was very little replacement of capital by labour in comparison with techniques used in investing countries." [63]

The scanty data in table 3.21 reflect the rapid increase in wages

63. Ibid., p. 193.

in Singapore. Since the consumer price index rose by less than 3 percent between 1967 and 1971, rising money wages also represent rising real wages. In the summer of 1972 almost every employer told me he was having difficulty getting Singaporean workers and was being forced to import workers from Malaysia. Rising money wages were not offset by changes in the exchange rate, which remained at $S3.06 per U.S. dollar from 1966 to mid-1971, when it appreciated to $S2.95 per U.S. dollar; by late 1972 it had appreciated to $S2.77 per U.S. dollar. Exporters have, therefore, had to rely on rising labor productivity (and appreciation of exchange rates or inflation in competing countries) to offset rising money wages.

Wages can be compared only for product E, where the local firm pays its female workers more than all three of the foreign firms and it pays its male workers about the average of the foreign firms.

It appears from the data in table 3.22 that most manufacturing

Table 3.22. Singapore: Previous Employment, by Number of Firms

| | Firms answering | Workers previously employed | | | |
		More than 50%	31–50%	11–30%	10% or less
Assembly					
Men					
Singaporean	3	0	1	0	2
Foreign	9	1	0	3	5
Women					
Singaporean	3	0	1	0	2
Foreign	9	1	0	5	3
Supervisory					
Singaporean	3	1	0	0	2
Foreign	6	1	1	1	3

Source: Questionnaires.

workers have no previous employment experience. Two-thirds of the firms reported that less than 30 percent of their supervisors had been previously employed, and over four-fifths of the firms reported that less than 30 percent of their assembly line workers had been previously employed. Only one firm (a foreign firm)

91449

reported that more than half its assembly line workers were previously employed. These results are quite similar to those for
South Korea.

Few of the previously employed workers had worked for foreign firms. Foreign firms are more likely than local firms to get
their experienced workers from other foreign firms (table 3.23).
This is also quite similar to the South Korean experience.

Table 3.23. Singapore: Workers Previously Employed by Foreign Firms
as Percentage of All Those Previously Employed

	Firms answering	More than 50%	31–50%	11–30%	1–10%	0%
Singaporean firms	2	0	0	0	0	2
Foreign firms	4	1	0	1	2	0

Source: Questionnaires.

The local firm is smaller than the foreign firm for all four
products (table 3.24). Output per worker is negatively correlated
with electricity consumption per worker for both product I and
product E.

A foreign company making product D and three of the companies making product E supplied monthly data on employment
and output. There is significant learning for two of the four firms.
The details of the statistical analysis of these data are in supplement 3.1.

Table 3.25 shows the rate of growth of output during 1969–71
for the five firms which answered this question. A comparison can
only be made for product I, where both the local firm and the
foreign firm experienced about the same decline in output.

A summary statement for Singapore must be even more quali-
fied than for South Korea, since the sample is smaller and many
of the firms have been operating for a shorter period of time. My
best generalizations are: (1) local firms have a slight tendency to
export more than foreign firms; (2) local firms buy at least as
much locally as foreign firms and occasionally buy more locally;
(3) there is no difference between local and foreign firms, on the
average, in ratio of value added to sales, in propensity to import,
or in degree of mechanization; (4) almost all firms are becoming

Table 3.24. Singapore: Average Monthly Output in 1971

	Per Worker	Total
Product A		
Singapore		
1[a]	191	17,750
Hong Kong		
1	40	45,750
2	n.a.	n.a.
Product E		
Singapore		
1[a]	970	32,996
Japan and		
Hong Kong		
1	1,483	440,332
2	898	591,983
Hong Kong		
1	504	377,950
Product G		
Singapore		
1	45	2,583
Hong Kong		
1	83	8,333
Product I		
Singapore		
1	8,315	582,064
Hong Kong		
1	9,766	2,343,733

[a] Based on partial year response.
Source: Questionnaires.

increasingly mechanized; (5) local firms are smaller than foreign firms; (6) local firms pay their workers more than foreign firms; (7) labor turnover is low, and foreign firms are more likely than local firms to get their experienced workers from foreign firms; and (8) output per worker is sometimes affected by learning.

TAIWAN

Because I collected the Taiwanese data in early 1973, some companies were able to supply data for 1972. The Taiwan sample in-

Table 3.25. Singapore: Annual Percentage
Rate of Growth of Output, 1969–71

Product A	
Singapore	
1	—
Hong Kong	
1	45
2	n.a.
Product E	
Singapore	
1	—
Japan and	
Hong Kong	
1	—
2	95
Hong Kong	
1	—
Product G	
Singapore	
1	—
Hong Kong	
1	42
Product I	
Singapore	
1	−11
Hong Kong	
1	−9

Source: Questionnaires.

cludes five local firms and ten foreign firms making products A,
C, E, F, J, and K. Product D was omitted because no foreign
firms made it, and products B and H were omitted because there
were no local firms in the sample. For four of the foreign firms
foreigners have 100 percent of the equity, and the foreigners'
share of the equity for the other six firms ranges from 40 percent
to 83 percent.

Thirteen of the sixteen firms have always exported their entire
output (table 3.26). While the foreign firm making product J
has experienced a rising proportion of exports, the foreign firms
making products A and E show no trend in the relative importance
of exports.

Table 3.26. Taiwan: Domestic Sales as Percentage of Total Sales

	1964	1965	1966	1967	1968	1969	1970	1971	1972
Product A									
Taiwan									
1	n.a.	n.a.	n.a.	n.a.	n.a.	n.a.	0	0	n.a.
Japan									
1	—	—	—	—	—	0	0	0	0
2	100	100	45	86	100	100	38	100	n.a.
3	n.a.	n.a.	n.a.	n.a.	n.a.	n.a.	0	0	n.a.
U.S.									
1	—	—	—	—	—	—	0	0	n.a.
Product C									
Taiwan									
1	—	—	—	—	—	—	0	0	n.a.
U.S.									
1	—	—	—	n.a.	n.a.	n.a.	n.a.	n.a.	0
Product E									
Taiwan									
1	—	—	—	—	—	—	n.a.	n.a.	n.a.
Japan									
1	—	—	—	—	—	—	—	—	100
Product F									
Taiwan									
1	—	—	—	—	—	0	0	0	n.a.
Japan									
1	—	—	—	—	—	—	0	0	0
Product J									
Taiwan									
1	0	0	0	0	0	0	0	0	n.a.
Japan									
1	—	—	—	—	—	—	0	0	n.a.
U.S.									
1	70	64	32	41	20	22	25	19	n.a.
Product K									
Taiwan									
1	—	—	—	—	—	—	0	0	n.a.
Japan									
1	—	—	—	—	—	0	0	0	n.a.
2	—	—	—	—	—	—	0	0	n.a.

Source: Questionnaires.

For products F and K the local firm imports more than the foreign firm. The data for the other three products (table 3.27) are too scanty to support any comparison.

For two products, J and K, foreign firms buy more from local firms than do local firms. On the other hand, for products A and F foreign firms buy less from local firms (table 3.28).

Foreign firms have a higher value added—wages plus local purchases—as a proportion of sales for products J and K and a lower proportion than local firms for product A (table 3.29).

One can compare mechanization for only four products: A, E, F, and J. Meager data (table 3.30) indicate that for three products, A, F, and J, foreign firms are more mechanized than local firms, with the exception of a very labor-intensive U.S. firm making product A. For product E the two firms are equally mechanized. Two of the three firms supplying at least four years' data show rising mechanization over time.[64]

These trends are consistent with the wage data (table 3.31). Of thirteen companies supplying wage data, eight had an annual increase between 1970 and 1971 in average annual female wages in excess of 5 percent. Daily earnings of factory workers in Taiwan rose an average of 8.5 percent annually between 1966 and 1970.[65] As the exchange rate has remained at $NT40.0 per U.S. dollar since 1963, exporters must offset rising money wages with higher productivity (supplemented by inflation in other countries). Foreign firms paid male and female workers less in both 1970 and 1971 than local firms for products A and K and more than local firms for product J.

Most assembly line workers have not been previously employed. The data in table 3.32 show that about 79 percent of the

64. Ranis, measuring capital by its value, reports that between 1965 and 1969 a large electronics company in Taiwan experienced a decline in its capital/labor ratio. Gustav Ranis, "Industrial Sector Labor Absorption," *Economic Development and Cultural Change* 21 (April 1973): 407. I suspect this decline is due to increased utilization of capital rather than adaptation of machinery. Reducing capital/labor ratios by increasing utilization rates can continue only for a few years. My data for this company indicate that its electricity consumption per worker tripled between 1967 and 1971.

65. *Industry of Free China* 38 (December 1972): 186.

Table 3.27. Taiwan: Value of Imports (excluding Tariffs and Fees)
Attributed to Exports as Percentage of Value of Exports

	1964	1965	1966	1967	1968	1969	1970	1971	1972
Product A									
Taiwan									
1	n.a.	n.a.	n.a.	n.a.	n.a.	n.a.	20	26	n.a.
Japan									
1	—	—	—	—	—	n.a.	n.a.	n.a.	n.a.
2	n.a.	n.a.	n.a.	n.a.	n.a.	n.a.	n.a.	n.a.	n.a.
3	n.a.	n.a.	n.a.	n.a.	n.a.	n.a.	35	30	n.a.
U.S.									
1	—	—	—	—	—	—	68	4	n.a.
Product C									
Taiwan									
1	—	—	—	—	—	—	17	38	n.a.
U.S.									
1	—	—	—	n.a.	n.a.	n.a.	n.a.	n.a.	153
Product E									
Taiwan									
1	—	—	—	—	—	—	n.a.	n.a.	n.a.
Japan									
1	—	—	—	—	—	—	—	—	—
Product F									
Taiwan									
1	—	—	—	—	—	44	58	52	n.a.
Japan									
1	—	—	—	—	—	—	n.a.	n.a.	6
Product J									
Taiwan									
1	n.a.	n.a.	n.a.	n.a.	4	n.a.	n.a.	n.a.	n.a.
Japan									
1	—	—	—	—	—	—	22	27	n.a.
U.S.									
1	2	2	2	6	7	7	5	4	n.a.
Product K									
Taiwan									
1	—	—	—	—	—	—	59	60	n.a.
Japan									
1	—	—	—	—	—	7	5	3	n.a.
2	—	—	—	—	—	—	n.a.	n.a.	n.a.

Note: The proportion of total imports attributed to exports is assumed equal to
the proportion of total sales that is exported.
Source: Questionnaires.

Table 3.28. Taiwan: Purchases from Taiwanese Firms (excluding Electricity) as Percentage of Value of Output

	1964	1965	1966	1967	1968	1969	1970	1971	1972
Product A									
Taiwan									
1	n.a.	n.a.	n.a.	n.a.	n.a.	n.a.	51	48	n.a.
Japan									
1	—	—	—	—	—	n.a.	n.a.	n.a.	n.a.
2	n.a.	n.a.	n.a.	n.a.	n.a.	n.a.	n.a.	n.a.	n.a.
3	n.a.	n.a.	n.a.	n.a.	n.a.	n.a.	43	46	n.a.
U.S.									
1	—	—	—	—	—	—	19	3	n.a.
Product C									
Taiwan									
1	—	—	—	—	—	—	23	18	n.a.
U.S.									
1	—	—	—	n.a.	n.a.	n.a.	n.a.	n.a.	n.a.
Product E									
Taiwan									
1	—	—	—	—	—	—	n.a.	n.a.	n.a.
Japan									
1	—	—	—	—	—	—	—	—	n.a.
Product F									
Taiwan									
1	—	—	—	—	—	14	17	31	n.a.
Japan									
1	—	—	—	—	—	—	n.a.	n.a.	1
Product J									
Taiwan									
1	15	17	9	8	5	5	6	6	n.a.
Japan									
1	—	—	—	—	—	—	91	53	n.a.
U.S.									
1	99	85	62	82	74	77	55	72	n.a.
Product K									
Taiwan									
1	—	—	—	—	—	—	7	9	n.a.
Japan									
1	—	—	—	—	—	84	83	87	n.a.
2	—	—	—	—	—	—	n.a.	n.a.	n.a.

Source: Questionnaires.

Table 3.29. Taiwan: Wages plus Local Purchases (including
Electricity) as Percentage of Value of Output

	1964	1965	1966	1967	1968	1969	1970	1971	1972
Product A									
Taiwan									
1	n.a.	n.a.	n.a.	n.a.	n.a.	n.a.	138	94	n.a.
Japan									
1	—	—	—	—	—	n.a.	n.a.	n.a.	n.a.
2	n.a.	n.a.	n.a.	n.a.	n.a.	n.a.	n.a.	n.a.	n.a.
3	n.a.	n.a.	n.a.	n.a.	n.a.	n.a.	52	55	n.a.
U.S.									
1	—	—	—	—	—	—	37	4	n.a.
Product C									
Taiwan									
1	—	—	—	—	—	—	n.a.	n.a.	n.a.
U.S.									
1	—	—	—	n.a.	n.a.	n.a.	n.a.	n.a.	n.a.
Product E									
Taiwan									
1	—	—	—	—	—	—	n.a.	n.a.	n.a.
Japan									
1	—	—	—	—	—	—	—	—	n.a.
Product F									
Taiwan									
1	—	—	—	—	—	17	21	34	n.a.
Japan									
1	—	—	—	—	—	—	n.a.	n.a.	n.a.
Product J									
Taiwan									
1	57	72	32	22	14	14	13	13	n.a.
Japan									
1[a]	—	—	—	—	—	—	121	60	n.a.
U.S.									
1	108	99	72	90	83	88	65	80	n.a.
Product K									
Taiwan									
1[a]	—	—	—	—	—	—	27	22	n.a.
Japan									
1[a]	—	—	—	—	—	92	90	94	n.a.
2	—	—	—	—	—	—	n.a.	n.a.	n.a.

[a] Excludes electricity.
Source: Questionnaires.

Table 3.30. Taiwan: Annual Electricity Consumption per Worker
(Kilowatt-hours)

	1964	1965	1966	1967	1968	1969	1970	1971	1972
Product A									
Taiwan									
1	n.a.	n.a.	n.a.	n.a.	n.a.	n.a.	390	290	n.a.
Japan									
1	—	—	—	—	—	405	744	820	742
2	n.a.	n.a.	n.a.	n.a.	n.a.	n.a.	n.a.	n.a.	n.a.
3	n.a.	n.a.	n.a.	n.a.	n.a.	n.a.	511	437	n.a.
U.S.									
1	—	—	—	—	—	—	5	2	n.a.
Product C									
Taiwan									
1	—	—	—	—	—	—	n.a.	n.a.	n.a.
U.S.									
1	—	—	—	953	1,947	2,475	4,672	2,994	2,617
Product E									
Taiwan									
1	—	—	—	—	—	—	41,606[a]	48,002	n.a.
Japan									
1	—	—	—	—	—	—	—	—	48,000[a]
Product F									
Taiwan									
1	—	—	—	—	—	20	26	39	n.a.
Japan									
1	—	—	—	—	—	—	n.a.	n.a.	276
Product J									
Taiwan									
1	1,181	860	1,000	773	926	1,080	1,095	906	n.a.
Japan									
1	—	—	—	—	—	—	n.a.	n.a.	n.a.
U.S.									
1	1,528	2,169	1,933	2,198	2,247	3,103	3,387	4,040	n.a.
Product K									
Taiwan									
1	—	—	—	—	—	—	n.a.	n.a.	n.a.
Japan									
1	—	—	—	—	—	n.a.	n.a.	n.a.	n.a.
2	—	—	—	—	—	—	378	430	n.a.

[a] Based on partial year response.
Source: Questionnaires.

Table 3.31. Taiwan: Average Annual Wages
(New Taiwan dollars)

| | Male | | Female | | Percentage change | |
	1970	1971	1970	1971	Male	Female
Product A						
Taiwan						
1	21,600	30,000	20,800	16,800	39	−19
Japan						
1	n.a.	n.a.	n.a.	n.a.	n.a.	n.a.
2	n.a.	n.a.	n.a.	n.a.	n.a.	n.a.
3	15,000	15,000	10,790	10,800	0	0
U.S.						
1	n.a.	10,140	9,620	10,210	n.a.	6
Product C						
Taiwan						
1	n.a.	n.a.	15,600	17,160	n.a.	10
U.S.						
1	n.a.	n.a.	n.a.	n.a.	n.a.	n.a.
Product E						
Taiwan						
1	33,330[a]	19,940	17,190[a]	20,320	−41	18
Japan						
1	—	—	—	—	—	—
Product F						
Taiwan						
1	4,680	4,680	11,940	10,940	0	−8
Japan						
1	n.a.	n.a.	n.a.	n.a.	n.a.	n.a.
Product J						
Taiwan						
1	19,520	17,140	5,450	6,300	−12	16
Japan						
1	20,110	20,440	10,540	10,610	2	1
U.S.						
1	20,570	24,360	16,070	17,020	18	6
Product K						
Taiwan						
1	24,760[a]	24,250	27,580[a]	24,600	−2	−11
Japan						
1	12,400	15,000	12,050	14,780	21	23
2	11,500	13,470	6,500	7,100	17	9

[a] Based on partial year response.
Source: Questionnaires.

Table 3.32. Taiwan: Previous Employment, by Number of Firms

| | Firms answering | *Workers previously employed* | | | |
		More than 50%	31–50%	11–30%	10% or less
Assembly					
Men					
Taiwan	7	2	0	1	4
Foreign	12	2	0	6	4
Women					
Taiwan	8	2	1	2	3
Foreign	12	4	1	3	4
Supervisory					
Taiwan	7	3	2	0	2
Foreign	12	6	0	1	5

Source: Questionnaires.

firms reported that less than 30 percent of their assembly line males were previously employed, and about 60 percent of the firms reported that less than 30 percent of their assembly line females were previously employed. Almost half the firms reported that over half their supervisory workers had been previously employed. These proportions of workers with previous employment are higher than for either South Korea or Singapore.

Taiwan also has a smaller proportion of industrial workers coming directly from the rural areas than does South Korea.[66] A non-random sample I made while touring twenty-six factories revealed that in Taipei 27 percent of assembly line females had fathers who were farmers, while in Hsin-chu, Kaohsiung, Tainen, and Taichung 64 percent of assembly line females had fathers who were farmers.[67]

Despite the greater labor mobility and urbanization of the labor force in Taiwan, one finds, as in Singapore and South Korea, that very few of the local firms' previously employed workers have worked for foreign firms (table 3.33). Forty percent of the local firms said that none of their experienced workers had worked for foreign firms, and another 40 percent of the local firms said that

66. Singapore, a city on an island, has no significant rural population.
67. My sample consists of twenty-two workers in Taipei and fourteen workers in the other four cities.

Table 3.33. Taiwan: Workers Previously Employed by Foreign Firms
as Percentage of All Those Previously Employed

	Firms answering	More than 50%	31–50%	11–30%	1–10%	0%
Taiwanese firms	5	0	1	0	2	2
Foreign firms	10	2	2	1	4	1

Source: Questionnaires.

less than 10 percent of their experienced workers had worked for foreign firms. The foreign firms were much more likely to have workers who had previously worked for foreign firms: 40 percent of the foreign firms said that at least 30 percent of their experienced workers had worked for foreign firms.

There are examples in Taiwan of local firms being aided in other ways by foreign firms. In both local transistor companies many of the top managers and technicians were trained by a U.S. firm that makes transistors in Taiwan. Both these local companies are new, and it is not clear that they will be able to generate large exports. One of the two local firms making television sets was initially a joint venture with a U.S. firm and in 1970 became wholly locally owned; many of its technicians and managers were trained by a U.S. producer of television sets. But this local firm is prohibited, under its current licensing agreement with a U.S. firm, from exporting television sets to the U.S. Singer, on the other hand, helped an older local sewing machine company improve the quality of its parts, and now the local company is a major exporter of sewing machines.

While direct foreign investment and licensing seem to have helped a small locally-owned electronics industry to develop in Taiwan, the experience of the People's Republic of China shows that these are not necessary conditions. After the withdrawal of Soviet aid in 1960, the People's Republic of China imported $207 million of electronic equipment from Japan, West Germany, the United Kingdom, France, and Switzerland. The number of major electronics plants rose from 60 in 1960 to 200 in 1971, producing such items as transistors, integrated circuits, radios, black and white television receivers and transmitters, and "an impressive assortment of radar, sonar, avionics, and missile and nuclear instrumentation for the military." [68] It is, of course, possible that Japanese and European firms would not have sold electronics equipment to Taiwan if not allowed to make investments in Taiwan. It is my guess, however, that Taiwan, even with only one-sixtieth the population of mainland China, would have been an attractive market to at least some electronics firms.

As shown in table 3.34, for products E, F, and J the local firm is larger; for products A and K the local firm is between the foreign firms in size.

Can learning explain some of the differences in output per worker that are shown in table 3.34? Supplement 3.1 contains regression results for six firms, including a Japanese firm making product L and a U.S. firm making product B, both of which are excluded from the rest of this chapter because there are no local producers. Learning is significant for two of these six firms.

The rate of growth of output between 1969 and 1971 can be compared only for product J, where the U.S. firm grew somewhat faster than the local firm (table 3.35).

In summary, for Taiwan I would make the following generalizations: (1) foreign firms tend to be more mechanized than local firms, and most firms are becoming increasingly mechanized; (2) foreign firms tend to import less than local firms; (3) there are no clear differences concerning propensity to export, purchases from local firms, value added as a percentage of sales, wages, or size of firm; (4) labor turnover is somewhat higher than in Singapore and South Korea, and foreign firms are more likely to get their previously employed workers from foreign firms; and (5) output per worker is sometimes affected by learning.

COMPARISON OF THE IMPACT OF FOREIGN FIRMS

Having looked at each developing country separately, I turn now to a comparison of the behavior of foreign firms in all three coun-

68. This paragraph is based on Philip D. Reichers, "The Electronics Industry of China," in *People's Republic of China: An Economic Assessment,* Joint Economic Committee, Congress of the United States (Washington, D.C.: U.S. Government Printing Office, 1972). The quotation is from page 86.

Table 3.34. Taiwan: Average Monthly Output in 1971

	Per worker	*Total*
Product A		
Taiwan		
1	38	23,333
Japan		
1	48	59,001
2	n.a.	n.a.
3	63	40,000
U.S.		
1	75	21,990
Product C		
Taiwan		
1	n.a.	n.a.
U.S.		
1	2,813	1,924,500
Product E		
Taiwan		
1	1,734	397,133
Japan		
1	n.a.	n.a.
Product F		
Taiwan		
1	44	24,634
Japan		
1	88	11,154
Product J		
Taiwan		
1	26	20,833
Japan		
1	24	5,752
U.S.		
1	25	6,631
Product K		
Taiwan		
1	138	9,650
Japan		
1	173	24,156
2	72	3,379

Source: Questionnaires.

Table 3.35. Taiwan: Annual Percentage Rate of
Growth of Output, 1969–71

Product A	
Taiwan	
1	n.a.
Japan	
1	15
2	n.a.
3	−11
U.S.	
1	—
Product C	
Taiwan	
1	—
U.S.	
1	4
Product E	
Taiwan	
1	—
Japan	
1	—
Product F	
Taiwan	
1	−30
Japan	
1	—
Product J	
Taiwan	
1	12
Japan	
1	—
U.S.	
1	20
Product K	
Taiwan	
1	—
Japan	
1	45
2	—

Source: Questionnaires.

tries. There are only two conclusions common to all three countries: 1. labor turnover is low, and local firms are less likely than foreign firms to obtain previously employed workers from foreign firms; and 2. monthly output per worker is usually affected by learning that follows a logistic curve.

Now look at the areas where there is variety in the behavior of foreign firms compared with local firms:

1. foreign firms are more likely than local firms to export in South Korea, less likely than they to export in Singapore, and tend to export about as much as local firms in Taiwan;

2. foreign firms have a greater propensity to import than local firms in South Korea, a lesser propensity to import in Taiwan, and a similar propensity to import in Singapore;

3. local firms usually buy as much and sometimes more than foreign firms from other local firms in Korea and Singapore but are similar to foreign firms in this respect in Taiwan;

4. foreign firms tend to be more mechanized than local firms in Taiwan, but in Singapore and South Korea there is no pattern;

5. almost every firm is becoming increasingly mechanized, except in South Korea;

6. value added as a proportion of sales is about the same for local and foreign firms in Taiwan and Singapore, but in South Korea local firms have a greater proportion of value added to sales than foreign firms;

7. in Singapore local firms tend to pay higher wages than foreign firms, but in South Korea and Taiwan there is no clear pattern;[69]

8. while local firms are smaller than foreign firms in Singapore, there is no clear pattern in Taiwan and South Korea.

The failure to reach similar conclusions for all three countries may be due to a different mix of products being produced by foreign firms in each country. Product A is the only one made by local firms and foreign firms in all three countries. Products C and

---

69. Mason found that U.S. firms pay more than local firms in the Philippines and Mexico. His firms all sell in the local market. Mason, "Choice of Technology," p. 353. Wells also found that foreign firms pay higher wages than local firms. The firms in his sample also sell only in the local market. Wells, "Economic Man," p. 323.

E are made by foreign firms in all three countries, but not always by local firms in my sample. Can we learn anything by focusing on these three products? There are eight foreign firms and four local firms making product A, six foreign firms and six local firms making product E, and six foreign firms and two local firms making C. So the sample consists of twenty foreign and twelve local firms scattered among the three countries. The following comparisons are based on the relevant tables from the three preceding sections (plus the data for one firm making product C in Singapore that was not included in the tables because there were no local producers).

Eight of the twelve firms making product A have always exported their entire production; one foreign firm sells mainly in the local market; and one foreign firm and two local firms both export and sell in the local market. There are no clear trends for the latter three firms. Seven of the eight firms making product C only export; the other firm is a foreign firm for which exports have become increasingly important. Eleven of the twelve firms making product E both export and sell in the local market; the other firm is foreign and so far has not exported; for all the local firms exports have become increasingly important over time, but this is true for only three of the six foreign firms. I conclude from these data that local firms have a slightly greater propensity to export than foreign firms.

What about propensity to import? For product A there is no clear difference between foreign and local firms and no clear trend over time. For products C and E the data are too meager to reach any conclusions.

For both product A and product C the local firm buys more from other local firms than does the foreign firm in all three countries. This is also generally true for product E.[70]

The local firm tends to have a higher ratio of value added to sales than the foreign firm for product A in all three countries. For product C this comparison can only be made for South Korea, where the local firm again has a higher ratio of value

70. The same pattern has also been found in Canada. *A Citizen's Guide to the Gray Report* by the editors of the Canadian Forum (Toronto: new press, 1971), p. 59.

added. For product E the local firm has a higher value added than the foreign firm in South Korea and a lower value added than the foreign firm in Singapore.

For all three products value added is higher in Singapore than in either South Korea or Taiwan. At first glance, this finding is consistent with neoclassical economic theory, since Singapore relies less on tariffs and import licensing than either South Korea or Taiwan; by maintaining an equilibrium exchange rate Singapore apparently encourages firms to substitute domestic factors of production for imports. A closer examination of the data shows that this higher value added is due entirely to higher wage payments in Singapore. Purchases from local firms are lower in Singapore than in the other countries for products A and C and about the same for product E. Since most of the output of these three products is exported, one may wonder how Singapore competes with South Korea and Taiwan if wages as a fraction of sales are higher in Singapore.[71] As discussed below, there are no large differences in the degree of mechanization between Singapore and the other two countries. One possible answer is that production of these products in Singapore will soon end as capitalists realize that larger profits can be made in other countries.[72] Another possible answer is that, as discussed in chapter 2, multinational firms will continue to accept lower profit rates for their Singapore factories because they wish to spread their production facilities among several countries as a way of reducing their worldwide risks.

Looking at the average annual wage for females, local firms pay more than foreign firms for product A in both South Korea and Taiwan; there are no data for Singapore. For product C the foreign firms pay more than the local firm in South Korea; there are no data for Singapore and Taiwan. For product E local firms pay

71. While output per worker is about the same in the three countries, there are differences in wages. In 1970 the average female annual wage for product E was, at current exchange rates, about $450 in Singapore, $380 in South Korea, and $425 in Taiwan.

72. A recent news story indicates that foreign firms are having difficulty attracting workers in Malaysia and are now considering expansion into Indonesia. "Electronics Firms Rush to Malaysia as Labor Gets Costly and Scarce Elsewhere in Asia," *Wall Street Journal*, 20 September 1973, p. 36.

more in Singapore and about the same in South Korea; there are no data for Taiwan. So one cannot generalize in the area of relative wages.

For product A foreign firms are more mechanized than local firms in Singapore and Taiwan and less mechanized than local firms in South Korea. For product C a comparison can be made only for South Korea, where the one local firm is in the middle of the four foreign firms in terms of mechanization. For product E the foreign firms bracket the local firms in South Korea; there are insufficient data for Taiwan and Singapore to compare foreign and local firms. The data are too scanty to say anything about trends in mechanization for these three products.

Because wages are much higher in Singapore than in either South Korea or Taiwan and capital is probably cheaper in Singapore, one would expect greater mechanization in Singapore than in the other two countries. But the data reveal no clear pattern for products A and C. For product E the one Taiwan plant is the most mechanized, and the Singapore plant tends to be somewhat less mechanized than the South Korean ones.[73]

To summarize the discussion of the three products produced in all three countries: (1) local firms are somewhat more likely to export than foreign firms; (2) local firms tend to buy more than foreign firms from other local firms; (3) local firms have a higher ratio of value added to sales than foreign firms; and (4) one cannot generalize on the relative propensity to import, the relative degree of mechanization, and relative wage rates. As noted earlier, labor turnover is low in all three countries, and foreign firms are more likely than local firms to obtain workers who have been employed by foreign firms.

It is difficult to generalize about whether the developing country gets greater indirect benefits from foreign investment when the foreign firms begin making items that are not being produced by local firms. In the case of television receivers in Taiwan and transistors in all three countries, local firms began production after the arrival of the foreign firms and gained some technical and managerial personnel from those foreign firms. None of the

73. For a further discussion of this point, see appendix A.

local transistor companies has, however, yet established a substantial export market, and the local television firms have almost no exports. As discussed earlier, the experience of the People's Republic of China suggests that there are other ways of establishing a domestic electronics industry. To confuse the subject still further, recall that Singer in Taiwan showed an existing local firm how to improve the quality of its sewing machines, thereby enabling the local firm to begin exporting large numbers of sewing machines.

CONCLUSION

I conclude from all these tables and arguments that, in a comparison of foreign investment with an expansion of local firms, neither the direct nor the indirect economic benefits of this type of foreign investment are very great, if they exist at all. By most indices foreign firms resemble local firms, and by a few indices foreign firms are less beneficial to the local economy than local firms. One might have hoped for a more dramatic conclusion.

The reader should remember that this conclusion is based on a sample of three particular Asian countries and on foreign firms that concentrate on exports. One cannot extend it either to other developing countries or to foreign firms that concentrate on the local market.[74] I turn now to other possible economic and noneconomic benefits to understand why the governments of these three developing countries seek foreign investors who export manufactures.

74. For a case study of the latter situation—foreign investment in the Argentina pharmaceutical industry—see J. Katz, "Importación de Tecnologia, Aprendizaje Local e Industrialización dependiante" (Buenos Aires: Instituto DiTella, 1972). See also Mason, "Choice of Technology," and Wells, "Economic Man."

STATISTICAL EVIDENCE ON LEARNING

Practice Makes Perfect

For a statistical analysis of learning, let

Y_t = output in physical units per worker in month t;

O_t = output in physical units in month t; and

X_t = cumulative output through month $t = \sum_{t=1}^{t} O_t$.

Then the equation for the logistic curve is:

$$Y_t = e^{a-b/X_t} \tag{3.1}$$

As cumulative output becomes very large, output per worker approximates e^a. The sign of a depends on the unit of measurement of output per worker; for example, a could be negative if output per worker were measured in millions of units and positive if it were measured in thousands of units.

Introducing monthly output as an additional explanatory variable to reflect any short-term economies of scale gives:

$$Y_t = e^{a-b/X_t} O_t{}^c \tag{3.2}$$

Taking logarithms to the base e transforms equation 3.2 to

$$\log Y_t = a - \frac{b}{X_t} + c \log O_t \tag{3.3}$$

The least squares regressions for equation 3.3 are shown in table 3.36 in the first line for each of the nine firms in South Korea which supplied monthly data. The second line under each firm adds the logarithm of time as a third explanatory variable in the logistic formulation.

Hirsch, in his study of machine tools,[75] used a functional form which permits continuous learning:

75. Werner Z. Hirsch, "Firm Progress Ratios," *Econometrica* 24 (April 1956): 136–43. Actually, Hirsch's dependent variable is labor per unit of output, or $1/Y$ in my notation. He also assumes no changes in the scale

$$Y_t = aX_t^b \tag{3.4}$$

Introducing monthly output again and taking logarithms gives:

$$\log Y_t = \log a + b \log X_t + c \log O_t \tag{3.5}$$

The third line under each firm in table 3.36 shows the results for equation 3.5, and the fourth line shows this functional form including the logarithm of time.

As preliminary analysis indicated serial correlation was present for four of the companies, the various equations were estimated in first differences.[76] Judging by the Durbin-Watson statistics, this transformation substantially reduced the serial correlation for three companies.[77]

The coefficient for the logarithm of time is negative in twelve of the eighteen regressions including time as a variable, and the coefficient is at least twice its standard error in only seven of the regressions, four times with a negative coefficient and three times with a positive coefficient. So in general the passage of time is not a significant variable in explaining output per worker for these companies.

Looking at the two alternative equations excluding time as an independent variable (lines 1 and 3), one notes that the coefficient for the logarithm of cumulative output (line 3 for each firm) is negative in six out of nine cases. A negative coefficient implies that output per worker falls as cumulative output increases. I regard this as implausible.[78] In the three cases where there is a positive coefficient at least twice its standard error, the logistic curve (line 1 for each firm) gives a better fit for product E (R^2 of .50 versus .36), a slightly inferior fit for Japanese firm 1 pro-

---

of production and so, in effect, estimates $1/Y = aX^b$. This equation is sometimes called the unit progress function, and the coefficient b is called the progress elasticity. The percentage decline in labor requirements per unit of output when cumulative output doubles is called the progress ratio.

76. In the logistic curve, the reciprocal of cumulative output is an independent variable, and so taking first differences implies changing the expected value of the coefficient b from negative to positive.

77. Hirsch does not report Durbin-Watson statistics but indicates ("Firm Progress Ratios," p. 139) that his regressions "left virtually no curvilinearity in the residuals."

78. Hirsch never obtained this result.

Table 3.36. South Korea: Estimation of Short-Term Learning Curves
(T ratios in parentheses)

	Constant	$\frac{1}{\text{Cumulative output}}$	Log output	Log time	Log cumulative output	R^2	F	D-W	Number of monthly observations
Product A									
Japan									
Firm 1									
(1)	-2.96	28.7	.79			.93	73.2	2.15	14
	(-4.55)	(.09)	(10.51)						
(2)	-2.59	-537.0	.77	-.10		.94	48.8	2.32	14
	(-3.43)	(-.80)	(10.01)	(-.97)					
(3)	-2.87		.80		-.02	.93	74.9	2.15	14
	(-5.10)		(11.35)		(-.50)				
(4)	-3.76		.78	-.20	.12	.93	46.6	2.24	14
	(-1.98)		(9.55)	(-.50)	(.43)				
Firm 2[a]									
(1)	-.03	106.1	.94			.83	135.6	1.86	59
	(-1.81)	(.53)	(16.5)						
(2)	-.02	-123.0	.94	-.20		.83	89.3	1.87	59
	(-.86)	(-.25)	(16.4)	(-.50)					
(3)	-.02		.95		-.15	.83	138.2	1.87	59
	(-1.0)		(16.6)		(-1.08)				
(4)	-.01		.98	1.48	-1.46	.84	97.7	1.80	59
	(.59)		(16.7)	(1.91)	(-2.09)				

Product C

	(1)	(2)	(3)	(4)	(5)				
Japan									
Firm 1									
(1)	5.17 (6.90)	−619.4 (−5.18)	.70 (6.39)			.90	41.5	2.01	12
(2)	2.98 (2.84)	−112.0 (−.5)	.90 (7.65)	.40 (2.52)		.95	46.3	2.28	12
(3)	.69 (.93)		.85 (10.34)		.38 (7.23)	.95	74.3	2.34	12
(4)	1.82 (.72)		.90 (6.33)	.29 (.47)	.15 (.31)	.94	45.3	2.20	12
Firm 2[a]									
(1)	−.01 (−.93)	18.1 (.16)	1.00 (32.2)			.99	526.4	1.83	15
(2)	−.002 (−.05)	−135.9 (−.25)	1.00 (30.8)	−.09 (−.29)		.99	324.2	1.87	15
(3)	−.01 (−.54)		1.00 (30.9)		−.01 (−.21)	.99	527.2	1.85	15
(4)	−.01 (−.53)		1.00 (25.5)	−.02 (−.09)	.01 (.03)	.99	322.3	1.83	15
U.S.									
Firm 2									
(1)	7.40 (19.1)	−161.8 (−4.97)	.13 (2.89)			.67	44.6	1.48	47
(2)	5.71 (10.5)	−149.8 (−5.28)	.46 (4.99)	−.40 (−3.96)		.76	44.9	1.01	47
(3)	5.43 (13.5)		.62 (5.17)		−.21 (−3.07)	.58	29.8	.70	47
(4)	1.58 (1.02)		.54 (4.61)	−1.67 (−2.57)	.65 (1.90)	.63	24.6	.65	47

Table 3.36—Continued

	Constant	1 Cumulative output	Log output	Log time	Log cumulative output	R^2	F	D-W	Number of monthly observations
Korea									
Firm 1									
(1)	7.36 (10.5)	-65.1 (-6.47)	.27 (2.27)			.96	189.0	2.62	19
(2)	4.03 (3.46)	-11.0 (-.60)	.73 (4.28)	.25 (3.24)		.98	204.3	1.80	19
(3)	3.13 (11.8)		.68 (11.9)		.21 (7.70)	.97	248.0	1.58	19
(4)	3.75 (12.4)		1.10 (7.37)	.81 (2.96)	-.39 (-1.89)	.98	248.2	1.51	19
Product E									
Japan									
Firm 1									
(1)	5.77 (10.16)	-19,268 (-4.29)	.01 (.24)			.50	11.8	2.27	27
(2)	5.76 (9.87)	-18,442 (-2.79)	.01 (.22)	.01 (.17)		.50	7.58	2.26	27
(3)	4.37 (7.50)		.03 (.65)		.08 (3.09)	.36	6.87	1.73	27
(4)	-1.86 (-.75)		-.01 (-.11)	-.76 (-2.58)	.70 (2.90)	.51	7.88	2.15	27

Product H
U.S.
Firm 1[a]

(1)	-.04 (-2.19)	3,135.5 (1.57)	.93 (13.5)			.85	91.9	2.16	35
(2)	-.02 (-.73)	-166.9 (-.03)	.92 (13.0)	-.25 (-.68)		.85	60.3	2.20	35
(3)	-.03 (-1.24)		.92 (13.1)		-.15 (-1.36)	.85	89.8	2.15	35
(4)	-.03 (-1.19)		.87 (10.8)	-.84 (-1.55)	.50 (1.15)	.86	63.4	2.26	35

Product K
U.S.
Firm 1[a]

(1)	-.02 (-1.24)	1,644.8 (3.49)	.85 (7.19)			.85	31.2	2.46	14
(2)	-.01 (-.36)	1,549.9 (1.30)	.86 (4.94)	-.03 (-.09)		.85	18.9	2.46	14
(3)	.03 (1.16)		1.01 (4.20)		-.33 (-2.14)	.78	19.2	2.15	14
(4)	.004 (.21)		.58 (2.33)	-1.39 (-2.68)	.87 (1.87)	.87	22.3	2.38	14

[a] First differences.
Source: Questionnaires.

Table 3.37. Singapore: Estimation of Short-Term Learning Curves
(T ratios in parentheses)

	Constant	$\frac{1}{\text{Cumulative output}}$	Log output	Log time	Log cumulative output	R^2	F	D-W	Number of monthly observations
Product D									
Hong Kong									
Firm 1[a]									
(1)	−.09	2.20	1.01			.95	323	1.55	39
	(−2.43)	(4.78)	(15.72)						
(2)	.03	2.47	1.25	−1.96		.96	270	1.70	39
	(.66)	(5.84)	(13.14)	(−3.09)					
(3)	−.03		1.07		−.34	.92	202	2.43	39
	(−.57)		(4.46)		(−1.39)				
(4)	.004		.99	−.70	−.19	.92	132	2.46	39
	(.05)		(3.51)	(−.52)	(−.49)				
Product E									
Singapore									
Firm 1[a]									
(1)	−.05	3.58	1.00			.999	9073	2.26	21
	(−3.54)	(21.05)	(67.24)						
(2)	−.07	3.85	1.00	.13		.999	6479	2.62	21
	(−3.67)	(15.81)	(69.49)	(1.51)					
(3)	.01		1.00		−.28	.997	3252	1.00	21
	(.61)		(38.46)		(−12.14)				
(4)	−.05		1.02	.53	−.38	.999	3788	1.91	21
	(−2.04)		(50.41)	(3.80)	(−11.80)				

							R^2	F	DW	N
Japan and Hong Kong Firm 1[a]										
(1)	−.003 (−1.17)	300.1 (.13)	1.00 (65.79)				.999	4996	2.14	17
(2)	.005 (1.03)	−5721 (−1.44)	1.02 (66.02)	−.07 (−1.79)			.999	3856	2.53	17
(3)	.0005 (.15)		1.03 (58.02)		−.02 (−1.47)		.999	5763	2.36	17
(4)	−.001 (−.45)		1.04 (54.49)	.12 (1.51)	−.10 (−1.85)		.999	4196	2.58	17
Hong Kong Firm 1[a]										
(1)	−.04 (−1.67)	−.07 (−.10)	.62 (7.80)				.98	915	1.90	39
(2)	.03 (1.13)	1.51 (1.87)	.87 (8.23)	−1.18 (−3.24)			.99	774	1.80	39
(3)	−.006 (−.24)		.98 (7.16)		−.36 (−2.61)		.98	1091	1.70	39
(4)	.01 (.50)		.88 (5.47)	−.45 (−1.16)	−.23 (−1.25)		.98	735	1.89	39

[a] First differences.

Source: Questionnaires.

Table 3.38. Taiwan: Estimation of Short-Term Learning Curves
(*T* ratios in parentheses)

	Constant	$\dfrac{1}{\text{Cumulative output}}$	Log output	Log time	Log cumulative output	R^2	F	D-W	Number of monthly observations
Product A									
U.S.									
Firm 1[a]									
(1)	−.06	−472.7	.97			.99	811	1.70	15
	(−1.88)	(−.22)	(39.6)						
(2)	−.18	1,338.3	.98	2.01		.99	537	1.83	15
	(−1.37)	(.46)	(38.4)	(.95)					
(3)	−.06		.98		−.003	.99	808	1.69	15
	(−1.43)		(37.9)		(−.03)				
(4)	−.18		.99	2.33	−.11	.99	553	1.89	15
	(−1.56)		(36.3)	(1.15)	(−.75)				
Product B									
U.S.									
Firm 2									
(1)	−1.93	82.9	.55			.95	62	2.12	10
	(−2.32)	(.21)	(6.27)						
(2)	−4.16	72.1	.97	−.81		.997	743	2.84	10
	(−14.3)	(.75)	(21.7)	(−10.6)					
(3)	−3.05		1.03		−.32	.994	563	1.32	10
	(−13.4)		(14.8)		(−7.34)				
(4)	−3.84		.98	−.63	−.08	.997	773	2.81	10
	(−12.1)		(19.2)	(−2.89)	(−.91)				

	(1)	(2)	(3)	(4)	(5)				
Product E									
Taiwan									
Firm 1									
(1)	−1.84	−27.3	.50			.99	896	1.46	30
	(−5.39)	(−6.03)	(10.1)						
(2)	−2.31	−22.8	.59	−.04		.99	614	1.22	30
	(−4.68)	(−4.03)	(7.15)	(−1.32)					
(3)	−4.11		.97		−.10	.98	603	.84	30
	(−23.3)		(18.9)		(−4.00)				
(4)	−3.92		1.07	.22	−.26	.98	396	.91	30
	(−12.7)		(7.17)	(.74)	(−1.19)				
Product F									
Taiwan									
Firm 1[a]									
(1)	−.01	1,660	.95			.77	73	1.42	47
	(−.77)	(.20)	(12.1)						
(2)	−.02	11,108	.96	.14		.77	48	1.44	47
	(−.83)	(.49)	(12.0)	(.45)					
(3)	−.01		.95		.005	.77	73	1.42	47
	(−.72)		(12.1)		(.05)				
(4)	−.01		.93	−.63	.63	.77	48	1.43	47
	(−.69)		(10.4)	(−.62)	(.62)				
Product K									
Taiwan									
Firm 1[a]									
(1)	.04	2,167	.97			.98	315	2.21	19
	(1.57)	(1.07)	(25.0)						
(2)	.006	6,643	.98	.33		.98	203	2.33	19
	(.11)	(1.00)	(24.3)	(.71)					

Table 3.38—Continued

	Constant	$\dfrac{1}{\text{Cumulative output}}$	Log output	Log time	Log cumulative output	R^2	F	D-W	Number of monthly observations
(3)	.04 (1.42)		.97 (24.0)		−.09 (−.74)	.97	303	2.16	19
(4)	.05 (1.32)		.97 (19.6)	−.12 (−.22)	.005 (.01)	.97	190	2.14	19
Product L									
Japan									
Firm 1[a]									
(1)	.0002 (.01)	−53,387 (−1.77)	.81 (5.52)			.82	20.9	1.58	12
(2)	.05 (.72)	−140,016 (−1.21)	.82 (5.45)	−.41 (−.78)		.84	13.5	1.77	12
(3)	−.02 (−.39)		.81 (5.01)		.17 (1.25)	.80	17.6	1.45	12
(4)	−.05 (−1.40)		1.12 (6.40)	4.15 (2.58)	−3.62 (−2.46)	.89	21.3	3.21	12

[a] First differences.

Source: Questionnaires.

ducing C (R^2 of .90 versus .95), and about the same fit for the Korean firm producing C (R^2 of .96 versus .97).

This discussion suggests that in general the logistic curve gives a more satisfactory explanation of learning. The R^2 for the logistic curve formulation (excluding time) ranges from .50 to .99 and the regressions are significant at the 1 percent level for all firms.[79]

The logarithm of output, which indicates economies of scale in monthly output, is very significant and positive for all firms except the Japanese firm producing E. Looking at the constant term and the coefficient of the reciprocal of cumulative output, which together indicate learning in the logistic curve formulation, reveals that learning is fairly significant for seven firms (all except Japanese firm 2 producing A and Japanese firm 2 producing C).

In Singapore a foreign company making product D and three of the companies making product E supplied monthly data on employment and output. The regression results for the learning curves for these four companies are shown in table 3.37. As preliminary analysis revealed the presence of serial correlation for all four companies, I used first differences which, judging by the Durbin-Watson statistics, eliminated this econometric problem. The coefficient for the logarithm of time is negative in five out of the eight cases and has a t ratio greater than 2.0 only once. So, as in the case of South Korea, the passage of time is not a significant variable in explaining output per worker.

Looking at the two alternative equations excluding time (lines 1 and 3), one notes that the coefficient for the logarithm of cumulative output is always negative. As argued above, I find this result implausible. So, again as in the case of South Korea, the logistic curve (line 1) gives the best explanation of learning. For all firms there are significant economies of scale, as shown by the positive coefficient for the logarithm of output. There is significant learning, as shown by the constant and the coefficient of

79. Hirsch does not report all his R^2's but indicates ("Firm Progress Ratios," p. 139) that in 17 out of 22 cases R^2 exceeded .72 and was never less than .35. He apparently did not examine whether a logistic curve would better fit his data.

the reciprocal of output, for two of the four firms, a foreign firm making product D and a local firm making product E.

Table 3.38 shows the regression results for six firms in Taiwan, including a Japanese firm making product L, which is excluded from the rest of this chapter because no local firm makes it. As in the cases of Singapore and South Korea, time frequently has a negative coefficient (six times out of twelve in the case of Taiwan) and rarely has a significant positive coefficient (one time out of twelve in the case of Taiwan). Excluding time, the logarithm of cumulative output has a negative coefficient four out of six times, and neither of the two positive coefficients has a t ratio greater than 1.25. The logistic curve (line 1) gives the best general fit, as in the case of South Korea and Singapore. Serial correlation is not a serious problem in the reported regressions for the logistic curve (four of which use first differences). Short-term economies of scale, as shown by the coefficient of the logarithm of output, are always significant, and learning, as shown by the constant and the coefficient of the reciprocal of cumulative output, is significant for two of the six firms, a U.S. firm making product B and a local firm making product E.

In summary, fourteen foreign firms and five local firms provided monthly data, and the regressions suggest that a majority of these firms—eight foreign ones and three local ones—experienced learning along a logistic curve.

4

Conclusions

We shall have to evolve
problem-solvers galore
since each problem they solve
creates ten problems more.
Hilmar Baunsgaard

OTHER BENEFITS OF FOREIGN FIRMS

Are foreign companies more immune than local companies to attempts by local government to influence corporate behavior? These attempts might be through the marketplace—by changing the money supply, for example—or through the local equivalent of "jawboning" or moral suasion. One might argue that foreign firms are more immune because they have more options than local firms, such as the possibility of borrowing from the parent company, either openly or by manipulating transfer prices for foreign trade. On the other hand, local firms may be watched less closely by the government. I have found no episodes where there was a major identifiable change in government policy which could then be correlated with changes in the behavior of foreign and local firms.

I also have little to say about the extent to which foreign firms are influenced by governmental policies in the nations where the parent firm is incorporated (Japan or the U.S., in my sample). This influence could cover such areas as monopoly formation, trade with countries considered to be enemies by the parent government, or response to the balance of payments regulations of the parent government. These are potentially important areas which have been well covered by other authors, and I have nothing to add to their discussion.[1]

Since most of the foreign firms in my sample have been operating for only a few years and since almost all the firms have experienced steady increases in exports, I cannot compare the stability of foreign firms with that of local firms. Such a comparison awaits a slump in world trade of the commodities produced by these firms.

As noted in chapter 3, in South Korea and Taiwan local firms were generally producing and exporting manufactured commodities prior to the arrival of the foreign firm. Transistors and television receivers were the two commodities produced and exported first by foreign firms in these nations. In Singapore the foreign firm was generally the first exporter of the commodity. Why do the governments of South Korea and Taiwan encourage foreign firms to establish subsidiaries to produce and export items which local firms are already exporting?

One possible answer is that government officials expected, at the time the decision was made, that foreign firms would bring large amounts of cheap capital or superior technology and management. These officials may not have foreseen how small the economic benefits would be (see chapter 3), or that developing countries could raise capital by selling international bonds. A second possible reason is that government officials believed that there were other commodities, sold mainly in the local market, which local firms could not produce as efficiently as foreign firms and that these foreign firms would recognize a favorable investment climate by the presence of a large number of foreign firms. According to this argument, foreign firms may bring substantial capital or superior technology and management only 10 percent of the time, but this 10 percent will occur only if the other 90 percent of the foreign firms are also operating in the developing country. While I am skeptical of this argument, I have no way to refute it.

1. Richard N. Cooper, *The Economics of Interdependence* (New York: McGraw-Hill Book Co., 1968), ch. 4; and Seymour J. Rubin, "The International Firm and the National Jurisdiction," in *The International Corporation,* ed. Charles P. Kindleberger, pp. 179–204 (Cambridge, Mass.: M.I.T. Press, 1970).

It may be that the principal reason for attracting foreign firms is political, not economic. Rather than worry about such matters as additional capital or superior technology, government leaders may think about the political impact of foreign firms. While the political impact is usually considered to be negative[2] (at least in Latin America), I think governments in these three Asian countries consider it to be positive. Based on my interviews, I think South Korean officials believe: (1) the U.S. government is less likely to impose quantitative restrictions on imports from South Korea if there are a substantial number of U.S. firms exporting from South Korea; (2) the U.S. government is more likely to protect South Korea from military invasion if there are a substantial number of U.S. firms in South Korea; and (3) U.S. firms are a countervailing force to the Japanese influence in South Korea.

Taiwanese officials seem to have analogous ideas. For example, a U.S. newspaper reported in mid-1973 that "aside from purely business considerations, the Nationalists clearly hope that heightened economic ties will contribute to inducing the United States to preserve diplomatic relations with Taiwan, despite Washington's interest in détente with Peking." [3] Taiwanese officials also believe that foreign investment reassures local investors: another newspaper report says that "the continued influx of American investments, both new projects and expansion of existing plants, has also been reassuring to the Taiwan business community." [4] This argument presumably rests on the idea that the multinational firm scans the world and invests in the most profitable countries (after adjusting for risk) and so offers a reliable guide to local investors. Local investors who follow multinational firms may in fact end up in risky economic situations because, as shown in chapter 2, a multinational firm may reduce its worldwide risk by making a very risky investment if that investment's risks are weakly correlated with the firm's risks in other countries. Local firms may not,

2. Part of the problem is that foreign businessmen tend to be too timid in their demands for policy changes that would accelerate growth in developing countries. See Albert O. Hirschman, *How to Divest in Latin America, and Why* (Princeton: Princeton University Essays in International Finance, no. 76, 1969).
3. *New York Times,* 23 July 1973, p. 7.
4. *New York Times,* 21 May 1973, p. 17.

of course, realize that a strategy which is good for a multinational firm is not always good for them.

TAX POLICY TOWARD FOREIGN FIRMS

Suppose that for some combination of economic and political reasons the government of a developing country wishes to stimulate the inflow of foreign corporate investment. What tax policies should the government adopt? As noted earlier, South Korea, Taiwan, and Singapore all offer foreign firms a five-year exemption from corporate income tax (and exemption from import duties for raw materials that enter into exports). One could argue that these tax exemptions have no real significance for the multinational firm because it would merely adjust its transfer prices if the developing country tried to tax its profits. Suppose, however, that profits cannot be completely eliminated through the manipulation of transfer prices. In this case, should the developing country grant a tax exemption to foreign firms?

Believing (or assuming?) that firms equate after-tax rates of return around the world,[5] economic theorists tend to argue that the level of corporate income tax in a particular small country will affect the inflow of foreign capital. In order to discourage competitive granting of tax exemption by various borrowing countries, economists frequently recommend that the taxes paid to the borrowing country by the foreign subsidiary be credited against the tax liability of the parent corporation to its government.[6]

Economists who have interviewed businessmen about their in-

5. See, for example, G. D. A. MacDougall, "The Benefits and Costs of Private Investment from Abroad: A Theoretical Approach," *Economic Record* 36 (March 1960): 17–18, reprinted in *Readings in International Economics*, ed. Richard E. Caves and Harry G. Johnson (Homewood, Ill.: Richard D. Irwin, 1968), pp. 175–76.
6. If the borrowing country is so large that the amount of foreign capital it attracts affects the interest rate it must pay, then a tax credit scheme will also prevent the borrowing country and the lending country from each trying to maximize its own income by imposing an optimum tax on foreign capital. See Koichi Hamada, "Strategic Aspects of Taxation on Foreign Investment Income," *Quarterly Journal of Economics* 80 (August 1966): 361–75.

vestments in developing countries tend to be very skeptical that reducing the corporate income tax attracts additional foreign investment. Hughes and You, based on a survey of 127 firms from six countries that invested in Singapore, find that "foreign investors, almost without exception, stated that taxation concessions . . . did not play a significant role, and for the most part played no role at all, in bringing them to Singapore." [7] Aharoni, based on a survey of thirty-eight U.S. firms that had made over a hundred decisions about direct foreign investment, concludes that "the granting of income tax exemption by foreign governments is not an important factor in foreign investment decisions." [8] Schreiber, in a study of twenty-two U.S. companies in Taiwan, finds that "while half of the reporting companies said that the tax concession was meaningful, none said that without it they would not have invested in Taiwan." [9]

One might think, at first glance, that the U.S. corporate tax law explains these responses, since it gives the U.S. parent corporation a tax credit for taxes paid by its foreign subsidiary on its repatriated earnings. Indeed, the manner in which this tax credit is computed for developing countries actually gives an incentive to the subsidiary to pay a tax to the developing country. Consider the example shown in table 4.1, where the tax rate in the U.S. is assumed to be 50 percent and where the subsidiary is assumed to repatriate immediately to the U.S. all its after-tax profits. In the case of the nondeveloping country, the parent company's total tax is independent of the tax set by the foreign country (provided it is below the U.S. tax rate).[10] In the case of a developing coun-

7. Helen Hughes and You Poh Seng, eds., *Foreign Investment and Industrialisation in Singapore* (Canberra: Australian National University Press, 1969), p. 183.

8. Yair Aharoni, *The Foreign Investment Decision Process* (Boston: Harvard University Graduate School of Business Administration, 1966), pp. 234–35.

9. Jordan Schreiber, *U.S. Corporate Investment in Taiwan* (Cambridge, Mass.: University Press, 1970), p. 75.

10. Noting this point and observing that tax rates tend to cluster about 50 percent, Caves concludes that "tax-induced distortions in the international allocation of equity capital are likely to be minor." Richard E. Caves, "International Corporations: The Industrial Economics of Foreign

Table 4.1. Hypothetical Taxes

	Developing country		Nondeveloping country	
	(1)	*(2)*	*(3)*	*(4)*
Subsidiary's profit	$100,000	$100,000	$100,000	$100,000
Tax rate in foreign country	30%	0%	30%	0%
Tax payment to foreign country	$30,000	$ 0	$30,000	$ 0
Dividends paid to U.S. parent	70,000	100,000	70,000	100,000
Tentative U.S. tax	35,000	50,000	50,000	50,000
Credit for foreign tax paid	21,000	0	30,000	0
Actual U.S. tax	14,000	50,000	20,000	50,000
Total tax payments	44,000	50,000	50,000	50,000

try, a special formula is used to calculate the tax credit,[11] and by this formula the firm's total tax payments are lower when it pays a tax to the developing country (compare columns 1 and 2 of table 4.1). With a U.S. tax rate of 50 percent, the parent firm's total tax payment is minimized when the developing country's tax rate is 25 percent.[12]

However, another feature of the U.S. corporate tax law reduces the parent company's delight in paying some tax to the developing country. The U.S. government taxes the profits of the foreign subsidiary of a U.S. company only when they are repatriated to the U.S. company. This deferral provision allows the U.S. parent to obtain, as a matter of right, an interest-free "loan" from the U.S. Treasury, with the maturity of the loan being continuously set by the company. The value to the company of such a loan, which may never be repaid and which the firm obtains without answering

---

Investment," *Economica* 38 (February 1971): 24. Caves ignores the impact of tax deferral, which I discuss below, and the low tax rates in developing countries.

11. For the developing country, the tax credit equals (repatriated profit divided by profit before foreign tax) times foreign tax. For column 1, this gives: tax credit = ($70,000/$100,000) × $30,000 = $21,000.

12. This paragraph is based on Robert Hellawell, "United States Income Taxation and Less Developed Countries: A Critical Appraisal," *Columbia Law Review* 66 (December 1966), esp. pp. 1394–97.

any questions from the lender, clearly exceeds the interest cost of a conventional long-term bond issued by the company.[13]

So the benefits to the U.S. multinational firm of tax exemption in a developing country depend on whether or not the firm plans to repatriate its subsidiary's earnings directly to the U.S. If the parent company plans to repatriate immediately, then the developing country can help the multinational firm by imposing a tax on its subsidiary's income. If the multinational firm does not plan to repatriate the subsidiary's earnings directly to the U.S., then the developing country helps the multinational firm by exempting its subsidiary's profits from taxation.

There is, obviously, no particular reason why the tax policy of a developing country should have as its objective the welfare of the multinational firm. Nor does it seem likely that the U.S. government will eliminate the deferral provision of its tax law.[14] One suspects that none of the three countries in my study has gained much, in its competition with the other countries, by offering tax exemption to foreign firms, since a tax concession by one country is soon matched by the other two. As a recent United Nations study put it, "The most urgent point at issue among the developing countries is that of competition among themselves for foreign investment."[15] This competition has recently spread beyond the three Asian countries I have examined. Malaysia and South Vietnam both offer up to ten years' tax exemption for foreign companies exporting manufactures.[16]

Even if a developing country uses tax incentives, it need not offer them to every foreign company. As argued in chapter 2, foreign firms have good reason to "follow the leader." Once a

13. For a discussion of this provision, see Lawrence Krause and Kenneth Dam, *Federal Tax Treatment of Foreign Income* (Washington, D.C.: The Brookings Institution, 1964).

14. Senator McGovern proposed this elimination in the 1972 Presidential election.

15. *Multinational Corporations in World Development* (New York: United Nations, 1973), p. 90.

16. "Electronics Firms Rush to Malaysia as Labor Gets Costly and Scarce Elsewhere in Asia," *Wall Street Journal*, 20 September 1973, p. 36; and Investment Law No. 4/72 (June 1972), as reported in *The Economy of South Vietnam*, ed. Patrick M. Boarman (Los Angeles: Center for International Business, Pepperdine University, 1973), pp. 111–19.

couple of foreign companies in a particular industry have been attracted by special incentives, others will probably follow without incentives. Nor need the incentives be for five years: the evidence from my sample indicates that production learning takes place rapidly in these countries, usually within a year.[17] Since the foreign companies usually sell to the parent company or another of its subsidiaries, there is no reason to subsidize them on the grounds that they need to be encouraged to learn about foreign markets.

One can only speculate on whether the governments of developing countries will be able to agree to impose a uniform tax on multinational manufacturing firms, and thereby increase the economic benefits they receive from the investments by these firms which are designed mainly for export.

17. Of the nineteen companies with monthly data, twelve attained maximum output per worker within a year, and only three required more than two years to achieve maximum output per worker.

Appendix A: Production Functions

As the style of analysis in chapter 3 reveals, I did not collect these data for the purpose of estimating production functions for each product. Some readers may, however, be interested in the results of such an exercise.

If we let Q_i = amount of product i, L_i = amount of labor used in making product i, and K_i = amount of capital used in making product i, then a production function frequently used by economists is:

$$Q_i = aL_i^b K_i^c \qquad a > 0, b > 0, c > 0 \qquad \text{(A 1)}$$

In my sample, L_i is measured by the number of workers for the firm during the year, K_i is measured by the firm's annual consumption of electricity (in kilowatt hours), and Q_i is the number of units of product i made by the firm during the year. Some firms have several years of data; others only a single year.

What if firms are not attaining maximum output for any given set of inputs? This problem has been considered by Aigner and Chu for data from the U.S.,[1] by Diaz-Alejandro for data on cement production in many countries,[2] and by Pack for data on bicycles, wheat milling, paint, tires, cotton spinning, and woolen yarns in five countries.[3] In order to see whether the failure to

1. D. J. Aigner and S. F. Chu, "On Estimating the Industry Production Function," *American Economic Review* 58 (September 1968): 826–38.
2. Carlos F. Diaz-Alejandro, "Labor Productivity and Other Characteristics of Cement Plants: An International Comparison," Yale University, Economic Growth Center Discussion Paper no. 117 (New Haven, July 1971). His data use physical measures for capital, labor, and output.
3. Howard Pack, "The Employment-Output Trade-off in LDC's—A Microeconomic Approach," Yale University, Economic Growth Center

achieve maximum annual output is serious for my data, I follow Diaz-Alejandro and Pack and calculate a unit isoquant. For each observation of output and inputs, I calculate electricity per unit of output and workers per unit of output. Diagram A.1 illustrates the results, using product K.

There are ten observations for three firms making product K. Perhaps the most remarkable thing about diagram A.1 is that most points are inefficient in the sense that they show a firm using more of both electricity and labor than at some other point. There are only two efficient points—points where the combination of electricity and labor is such that reducing the amount of either input requires an increase in the amount of the other input.[4] The line connecting these efficient points is KK and can be considered an efficient isoquant.

How does one explain the fact that 80 percent of the observations for product K are inefficient? One possibility is that, over time, firms approach the efficient isoquant. For example, one can see that between 1965 and 1970 firm 1 (shown by dots) converged on an efficient capital-intensive production technique; firm 2 (shown by x's) moved to an efficient labor-intensive technique in two years. For other products most firms do not seem to be converging on the efficient isoquant. While all these firms are selling mainly in world markets, it still may be true that they are not driven by competition to the most efficient production technique.[5] For products produced by multinational firms, world markets may not be very competitive. Another possible explanation is that I have ignored economies of scale or other inputs, such as management or skilled labor, that are important in explaining differences among firms' ratios of employment to output and capital to output.

Discussion Paper no. 179 (New Haven: June 1973). Pack's data consist of man-hours for labor, estimated replacement cost for machinery (at official exchange rates) for capital, and value added (at official exchange rates) for output.

4. Pack also found that there were often only two efficient points (ibid., p. 6).

5. For a theoretical model along these lines, see Richard R. Nelson and Sidney G. Winter, "Toward an Evolutionary Theory of Economic Capabilities," *American Economic Review* 63 (May 1973): 440–49.

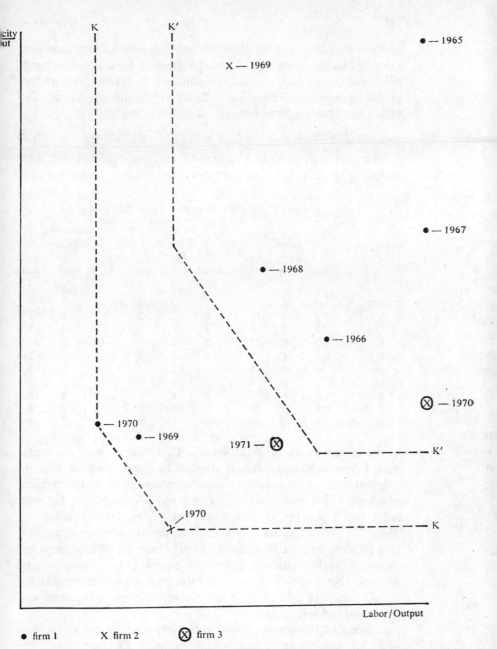

Diagram A.1. Unit Isoquant

Since I want to see whether foreign firms have a different production function than local firms, I introduce as a third independent variable a dummy variable in equation A.1; taking logarithms in this equation gives equation A.2, where the dummy has a value of 1 if the firm is a local firm and 0 if it is a foreign firm.

$$\log Q_i = \log a + b \log L_i + c \log K_i + d \,(\text{dummy}) \qquad (A.2)$$

I need at least five observations to estimate equation A.2, but, as shown in table A.1, there are only two efficient points for nine

Table A.1. Number of Observations for Production Functions

Product	Initial Local	Initial For-eign	Initial Total	Efficient Local	Efficient For-eign	Efficient Total	Reasonably Efficient Local	Reasonably Efficient For-eign	Reasonably Efficient Total
A	5	14	19	0	3	3	2	5	7
B	0	4	4	0	2	2	0	3	3
C	2	14	16	0	2	2	2	8	10
D	5	0	5	2	0	2	5	0	5
E	10	15	25	1	1	2	10	8	18
F	3	1	4	1	1	2	1	1	2
G	0	5	5	0	2	2	0	5	5
H	2	3	5	2	0	2	2	3	5
I	8	8	16	0	1	1	8	8	16
J	8	8	16	2	0	2	5	3	8
K	6	4	10	1	1	2	2	2	4

of the eleven products. What should I do? To remedy this situation, I have arbitrarily drawn another isoquant, such as K'K' in diagram A.1, which is twice as far from the origin as the efficient isoquant, and I include in the regression all the points between these two isoquants. I call these points "reasonably efficient." Thus, for product K there are four observations that are reasonably efficient and six that are not. I then use the observations for these reasonably efficient points to estimate, by ordinary least squares, equation A.2. Line 1 of table A.2 shows the results for the six products with at least five reasonably efficient points and both local and foreign firms.

Because of the small sample size, only four of the six regressions are significant at the 5 percent level. Of these four, the nationality dummy variable (column 2) has a *t* ratio with absolute value greater than 2.0 for products C, I, and J. The coefficient for nationality is negative for products C and I, which indicates the local firms are less efficient, all other things equal, than the foreign firms; for product J the coefficient is positive, indicating the local firm is more efficient than the foreign firm.

The coefficients for the logarithms of labor and electricity (columns 3 and 4) both have *t* ratios in excess of 2.0 only for products C and E. The labor coefficient for the logarithm of labor is negative for product I, which is implausible. For products C and E, the summations of the two coefficients for labor and electricity are .93 and .88 respectively, which suggests that there are no economies of scale for these two products.

As noted above, a possible explanation for so many inefficient observations is that firms are learning and are approaching the efficient isoquant. I find this unlikely, since the learning curves, estimated with monthly data in chapter 3, show that the majority of companies attain maximum output per worker within a year. To test the learning hypothesis directly with these annual data, I introduce another dummy variable, age, which takes a value of zero if the firm has been operating less than three years and one if the firm has been operating for at least three years. The results of this regression are shown in line 2 of table A.2 for five products for the reasonably efficient observations and in table A.3 for six products for all the observations.

The coefficient on the age dummy never has a *t* ratio with an absolute value greater than 1.0 for the three significant regressions for the reasonably efficient observations. Using all the observations, there are significant regressions for products A, E, I, and J. Looking at the two products with significant coefficients on the age dummy, old firms are more productive for product E and less productive for product J. So, in general, the annual data are consistent with the monthly data: there is little learning after the first two years. The coefficient on the nationality dummy using all the observations indicates that local firms are less productive for product I and more productive for product J. These results are consistent with those obtained using only the reasonably efficient observations. Notice that, in regressions using all the data,

Table A.2. Regressions for Reasonably Efficient Production Function
(T ratios in parentheses)

Product	Constant (1)	Nationality dummy (2)	Log labor (3)	Log electricity (4)	Age dummy (5)	R^2 (6)	F (7)	Observations (8)
A								
(1)	2.79 (1.17)	−.28 (−.62)	1.54 (3.29)	.14 (1.86)		.87	6.41*	7
(2)	2.54 (1.68)	.02 (.07)	1.53 (5.18)	.19 (3.62)	−.64 (−2.35)	.96	13.4*	7
C								
(1)	1.03 (1.06)	−.67 (−4.23)	.40 (3.71)	.53 (4.70)		.99	391	10
(2)	1.11 (.99)	−.68 (−3.88)	.41 (3.10)	.51 (3.85)	−.05 (−.22)	.995	247	10
E								
(1)	6.16 (5.51)	−.13 (−1.20)	.45 (5.74)	.43 (4.64)		.95	81.3	18
(2)	8.40 (5.02)	.15 (.75)	.29 (1.66)	.33 (2.16)	.22 (.84)	.84	16.9	18
H								
(1)	5.39 (3.08)	.36 (.89)	.31 (.30)	.49 (.73)		.98	20.8*	5
I								
(1)	−6.93 (8.58)	−.42 (−2.45)	−.04 (−.32)	1.20 (20.0)		.996	983	16

(2)	−7.30 (−7.18)	−.40 (−2.22)	−.04 (−.29)	1.22 (16.9)	−.02 (−.63)	.996	699	16

J

(1)	−14.1 (−5.87)	1.59 (3.60)	.26 (.63)	1.72 (7.08)		.99	140	8
(2)ᵃ	−65,249 (−.00)	1.79 (.32)	−1.34 (−.26)	−1.34 (−.48)	65,286 (.00)	−.13	−.08	8

* Not significant at 5 percent.

ᵃ Negative R² because of dummy variable.

Table A.3. Regressions for Production Functions
(*T* ratios in parentheses)

Product	Constant	Nationality dummy	Log labor	Log electricity	Age dummy	R^2	F	Observations
A	8.06	−.32	.58	.08	.01	.66	6.77	19
	(8.83)	(−.73)	(2.98)	(1.01)	(.03)			
C	−10.71	.77	−.89	1.86	−.43	.43	2.10*	16
	(−1.18)	(.43)	(−.89)	(1.83)	(−.40)			
E	3.73	.04	−.12	.77	.75	.83	24.0	25
	(2.19)	(.19)	(−.58)	(4.95)	(2.51)			
I	−7.30	−.40	−.04	1.22	−.02	.996	699	16
	(−7.18)	(−2.20)	(−.29)	(16.9)	(−.63)			
J	−6.42	.55	1.01	.89	−.44	.98	110	16
	(−3.43)	(2.10)	(3.99)	(3.86)	(−2.18)			
K	−5.50	−4.00	1.30	1.09	1.55	.58	1.75*	10
	(−.33)	(−1.27)	(.62)	(.53)	(1.01)			

* Not significant at 5 percent.

the coefficients for the logarithms of labor and electricity occasionally have negative signs and only a minority have *t* ratios in
excess of 2.0. Perhaps a more sophisticated analysis, trying alternative functional forms and using more dummy variables, would
give better regression results.

What can one learn looking only at the efficient observations?
There is not much systematic difference between local and foreign firms. As shown in table A.1, for five products all the efficient observations are by foreign firms; for three products all the
efficient observations are by local firms; and for three products
one efficient observation is by a foreign firm and one by a local
firm.

One can also compute the ratio of the percentage change in
labor to the percentage change in electricity along the efficient
isoquant between the two efficient points.[6] The results are shown

6. This is not the elasticity of substitution, which is the percentage
change in the capital/labor ratio divided by the percentage change in the
ratio of the price of capital to the price of labor. See, for example, Edwin
Mansfield, *Microeconomics* (New York: W. W. Norton and Co., 1970),

Table A.4. Ratio of Percentage Change in Labor to Percentage
Change in Capital Along Efficient Isoquant

Product

A	−.07
B	−2.5
C	−2.4
D	−.45
E	−2.4
F	−.03
G	−475
H	−.07
J	−1.1
K	−.07

in table A.4. While some of the results seem implausible—could employment increase by 475 percent when electricity consumption falls by 1 percent, as indicated for product G?—there does seem to be scope for a fair amount of substitution of labor for capital for products B, C, and E. There is much less scope for substituting labor for capital for products A, D, F, H, J, and K.

In summary, a simple formulation of a production function implies that most firms fail to maximize output for a given set of inputs, and this failure does not seem to be due to the inexperience of the firms. In the few cases where one can obtain a significant regression, there is no systematic difference between foreign and local firms. For the majority of products in my sample there is little scope for substituting labor for capital.

p. 356. I have no data on the differences in the cost of capital among the various efficient firms, and I have no reason to think it is the same for both local and foreign firms in three different developing countries.

Appendix B: Questionnaire

This is a copy of the questionnaire that was used in Taiwan, except that each line was also translated into Chinese. The South Korean and Singaporean questionnaires were similar but were only in English.

PLEASE FILL OUT ONE FORM FOR EACH PLANT.

Name of Company Owning Plant _____

Address of Plant _____

Product Produced _____

First Year of Production _____

What Percentage of Equity of Company is Owned by Foreigners?

_____

FOR EACH YEAR, PLEASE ANSWER AS MANY AS POSSIBLE:
Value should be in thousand NT dollars unless otherwise stated.

	1971 (1)	1970 (2)	1969 (3)	1968 (4)	1967 (5)	1966 (6)	1965 (7)	1964 (8)	Earlier Years (9)
1. *OUTPUT*									
A. Physical units (specify)	—	—	—	—	—	—	—	—	—
B. Value (thousand NT$)	—	—	—	—	—	—	—	—	—

	1971 (1)	1970 (2)	1969 (3)	1968 (4)	1967 (5)	1966 (6)	1965 (7)	1964 (8)	Earlier Years (9)
2. SALES									
A. Domestic									
(i) Physical units	—	—	—	—	—	—	—	—	—
(ii) Value (thousand NT$)	—	—	—	—	—	—	—	—	—
B. Export									
(i) Physical units	—	—	—	—	—	—	—	—	—
(ii) Value (thousand NT$)	—	—	—	—	—	—	—	—	—
3. LABOR									
A. Average Number Employed during Year									
(i) Male	—	—	—	—	—	—	—	—	—
(ii) Female	—	—	—	—	—	—	—	—	—
B. Total Wages (Value in thousand NT$)									
(i) Male	—	—	—	—	—	—	—	—	—
(ii) Female	—	—	—	—	—	—	—	—	—
4. ELECTRICITY									
A. Purchased									
(i) Amount (kilowatt-hours)	—	—	—	—	—	—	—	—	—
(ii) Value (thousand NT$)	—	—	—	—	—	—	—	—	—
B. Generated in Plant Amount (kilowatt-hours)	—	—	—	—	—	—	—	—	—
5. HORSEPOWER CAPACITY OF MACHINERY AND EQUIPMENT IN PLANT (excluding heating and air conditioning)	—	—	—	—	—	—	—	—	—

	1971 (1)	1970 (2)	1969 (3)	1968 (4)	1967 (5)	1966 (6)	1965 (7)	1964 (8)	Earlier Years (9)

6. *PURCHASES OTHER THAN ELECTRICITY— VALUE*
   A. From Taiwan firms (thousand NT$)
   B. Imports
      (i) including tariffs and other fees (thousand NT$)
      (ii) excluding tariffs and other fees (thousand NT$)

7. *NUMBER OF EMPLOYEES*
   A. Nationals
      (i) With university & college degree
      (ii) Secondary school degree
      (iii) Less than secondary degree
   B. Foreigners
      (i) With university & college degree
      (ii) Secondary school degree
      (iii) Less than secondary degree

8. For each *month* since beginning of production, please list (i) output in physical units, (ii) total number of persons employed, and (iii) total consumption of electricity in Kilowatt-hours. This information can be provided on a separate page.

9. Approximately what percentage of labor force is paid on piece-rate basis? _____

10. About what percentage of the women in "assembly line" labor force had previously worked in a factory before being employed by your firm? ______ Percentage of men in "assembly line"? ______ Percentage of "supervisory personnel?" ______ Of those who had worked in a factory before, what percentage had worked in a company owned entirely or partly by foreigners? ______

Bibliography

BOOKS, ARTICLES, AND UNPUBLISHED PAPERS

Aharoni, Yair. *The Foreign Investment Decision Process.* Boston: Harvard University Graduate School of Business Administration, 1966.

Aigner, D. J., and Chu, S. F. "On Estimating the Industry Production Function." *American Economic Review* 58 (September 1968): 826–38.

"The Americanization of Sony." *New York Times,* 18 March 1973, sec. 3, p. 1.

Arpan, Jeffrey. *International Intracorporate Pricing: Non-American Systems and Views.* New York: Praeger, 1971.

Arrow, Kenneth J. "The Economic Implications of Learning by Doing." *Review of Economic Studies* 29 (June 1962): 155–73.

———. "Uncertainty and the Welfare Economics of Medical Care." *American Economic Review* 53 (December 1963): 941–73.

Baerresen, Donald. *The Border Industrialization Program of Mexico.* Lexington, Mass.: D. C. Heath and Co., 1971.

Bancroft, Gertrude, and Garfinkle, Stuart. "Job Mobility in 1961." *Monthly Labor Review* 86 (August 1963): 897–906.

Baran, Paul A. "On the Political Economy of Backwardness." *The Manchester School* 20 (January 1952). Reprinted in *The Economics of Underdevelopment,* edited by A. N. Agarwala and S. P. Singh. Oxford: Oxford University Press paperback, 1958.

Becker, Gary S. "Investment in On-the-Job Training." In *Economics of Education,* edited by M. Blaug, vol. 1. Baltimore: Penguin Books, 1968.

Berg, Ivar. *Education and Jobs: The Great Training Robbery.* New York: Praeger, 1971.

Boarman, Patrick M., ed. *The Economy of South Vietnam.* Los Angeles: Center for International Business, Pepperdine University, 1973.

Bowles, S., and Levin, H. "The Determinants of Scholastic Achievements—An Appraisal of Some Recent Evidence." *Journal of Human Resources* (Winter 1968), pp. 3–24.

155

Brainard, William C., and Cooper, Richard N. "Uncertainty and Diversification in International Trade." *Studies in Agricultural Economics, Trade, and Development* 8 (1968): 257–85.
Brecher, Richard A. "Disguised Versus Open Unemployment: A Trade-Off." Mimeographed. New Haven, 1971.
Bruck, Nicholas K., and Lees, Francis A. *Foreign Investment, Capital Controls, and the Balance of Payments.* New York University Institute of Finance Bulletin no. 48–49. New York, 1968.
"Canada Announces Plans to Curb Foreign Business." *New York Times,* 3 May 1972, p. 1.
Casas, Juan Carlos. "Las Multinacionales y el Comercio Latinoamericano." *Cemla Boletin Mensual* 18 (December 1972): 605–14.
Caves, Richard E. "International Corporations: The Industrial Economics of Foreign Investment." *Economica* 38 (February 1971): 1–27.
———, and Jones, Ronald W. *World Trade and Payments: An Introduction.* Boston: Little, Brown and Co., 1973.
A Citizen's Guide to the Gray Report by the editors of the Canadian Forum. Toronto: new press, 1971.
Cohen, Benjamin I., and Ranis, Gustav. "The Second Postwar Restructuring." In *Government and Economic Development,* edited by Gustav Ranis, pp. 431–69. New Haven: Yale University Press, 1971.
Cohen, Benjamin I., and Sisler, Daniel G. "Exports of Developing Countries in the 1960's." *Review of Economics and Statistics* 53 (November 1971): 354–61.
"Competitor Emerging South of the Border." *Industry Week,* 2 October 1972, pp. 31–34.
Cooper, Richard N. *The Economics of Interdependence.* New York: McGraw-Hill Book Co., 1968.
———. "The European Community's System of Generalized Tariff Preferences: A Critique." *Journal of Development Studies* 8 (July 1972): 379–94.
Deese, James, and Hulse, Steward. *The Psychology of Learning.* 3rd ed. New York: McGraw-Hill Book Co., 1967.
Diaz-Alejandro, Carlos F. "Colombian Imports and Import Controls in 1970/71: Some Quantifiable Features." Yale University, Economic Growth Center Discussion Paper no. 182. New Haven, 1973.
———. "Direct Foreign Investment in Latin America." In *The International Corporation,* edited by Charles P. Kindleberger. Cambridge: M.I.T. Press, 1970.
———. "Labor Productivity and Other Characteristics of Cement Plants: An International Comparison." Yale University, Economic Growth Center Discussion Paper no. 117. New Haven, 1971.
Dougherty, Christopher, and Selowsky, Marcelo. "Measuring the

Effects of the Misallocation of Labour." *Review of Economics and Statistics* 55 (August 1973): 386–93.

Duesenberry, James. *Business Cycles and Economic Growth.* New York: McGraw-Hill Book Co., 1958.

Eckaus, Richard S. "Comment on Becker's Analysis of On-the-Job Training." In *Economics of Education,* edited by M. Blaug, vol. 1. Baltimore: Penguin Books, 1968.

The Effects of United States and Other Foreign Investments in Latin America. New York: The Council for Latin America, 1970.

The Effects of United States Corporate Foreign Investment 1960–1970. New York: Business International Corporation, 1972.

"Electronics Firms Rush to Malaysia as Labor Gets Costly and Scarce Elsewhere in Asia." *Wall Street Journal,* 20 September 1973, p. 36.

Evenson, Robert. "International Diffusion of Agrarian Technology." *Journal of Economic History* 36 (March 1974): 51–73.

Fei, John C. H., and Ranis, Gustav. *Development of the Labor Surplus Economy: Theory and Policy.* Homewood, Ill.: Richard D. Irwin, 1964.

Festinger, Leon. *A Theory of Cognitive Dissonance.* Stanford, Cal.: Stanford University Press, 1957.

Fisher, I. N., and Hall, G. R. "Risk and Corporate Rates of Return." *Quarterly Journal of Economics* 83 (February 1969): 79–92.

Frankena, Mark. "Restrictions on Exports by Foreign Investors: The Case of India." *Journal of World Trade Law* 6 (September–October 1972): 575–93.

Galbraith, John Kenneth. *The Affluent Society.* Boston: Houghton Mifflin Co., 1958.

———. *The New Industrial State.* Boston: Houghton Mifflin Co., 1967.

Grabowski, Henry C., and Mueller, Dennis C. "Managerial and Stockholder Welfare Models of Firm Expenditures." *Review of Economics and Statistics* 54 (February 1972): 9–24.

Grubel, Herbert G. "Internationally Diversified Portfolios: Welfare Gains and Capital Flows." *American Economic Review* 58 (December 1968): 1299–1314.

Hamada, Koichi. "Strategic Aspects of Taxation on Foreign Investment Income." *Quarterly Journal of Economics* 80 (August 1966): 361–75.

Hellawell, Robert. "United States Income Taxation and Less Developed Countries: A Critical Appraisal." *Columbia Law Review* 66 (December 1966): 1393–1427.

Helleiner, G. K. "Manufactured Exports from Less-Developed Countries and Multinational Firms." *Economic Journal* 83 (March 1973): 21–47.

————. "Manufacturing for Export: Multinational Firms and Economic Development." *World Development* 1 (July 1973): 13–21.

Hirsch, Seev, and Lev, Baruch. "Sales Stabilization Through Export Diversification." *Review of Economics and Statistics* 53 (August 1971): 270–77.

Hirsch, Werner Z. "Firm Progress Ratios." *Econometrica* 24 (April 1956): 136–43.

Hirschman, Albert O. *How to Divest in Latin America, and Why.* Princeton: Princeton University, Essays in International Finance, no. 76, 1969.

Ho, Yhi-Min. "Development with Surplus Population—The Case of Taiwan: A Critique of the Classical Two-Sector Model, à la Lewis." *Economic Development and Cultural Change* 20 (January 1972): 210–34.

Horst, Thomas. "Firm and Industry Determinants of the Decision to Invest Abroad: An Empirical Study." *Review of Economics and Statistics* 54 (August 1972): 258–66.

"How Risky Has Euroaid Been?" *The Economist* 249 (15 December 1973): 68–69.

Hughes, Helen, and You Poh Seng, eds. *Foreign Investment and Industrialisation in Singapore.* Canberra: Australian National University Press, 1969.

Hymer, Stephen. "The Efficiency (Contradictions) of Multinational Corporations." *American Economic Review* 60 (May 1970): 441–48.

————. "The International Operations of National Firms: A Study of Direct Foreign Investment." Ph.D. dissertation, M.I.T., 1960.

————, and Resnick, Stephen. "International Trade and Uneven Development." In *Trade, Balance of Payments, and Growth,* edited by Jagdish Bhagwati, Ronald Jones, Robert Mundell, and Jaroslav Vanek. Amsterdam: North-Holland Publishing Co., 1971.

Johnson, Harry G. "The Efficiency and Welfare Implications of the International Corporation." In *The International Corporation,* edited by Charles P. Kindleberger. Cambridge: M.I.T. Press, 1970.

Katz, J. "Importación de Tecnologia, Aprendizaje Local e Industrialización dependiante." Buenos Aires: Instituto DiTella, 1972.

————. "Technology, Dynamic Comparative Advantages and Bargaining Power." Mimeographed. Buenos Aires: Instituto DiTella.

Keynes, John Maynard. *Essays in Persuasion.* London: Rupert Hart-Davis, 1952.

Kindleberger, Charles P. *American Business Abroad.* New Haven: Yale University Press, 1969.

Knickerbocker, Frederick T. *Oligopolistic Reaction and Multinational Enterprise.* Boston: Harvard University Graduate School of Business Administration, 1973.

Krause, Lawrence, and Dam, Kenneth. *Federal Tax Treatment of Foreign Income*. Washington, D.C. The Brookings Institution, 1964.

Kuhn, Thomas. *The Structure of Scientific Revolutions*. 2d ed. Chicago: University of Chicago Press paperback, 1970.

Leff, Nathaniel. *The Brazilian Capital Goods Industry, 1929–1964*. Cambridge: Harvard University Press, 1968.

Lenin, V. I. *Imperialism: The Highest Stage of Capitalism*. New York: International Publishers, 1970.

Leontief, Wassily. "Domestic Production and Foreign Trade. The American Capital Position Re-Examined." *Economia Internazionale* 7 (February 1954): 3–32.

Levy, Haim, and Sarnat, Marshall. "International Diversification of Investment Portfolios." *American Economic Review* 60 (September 1970): 668–75.

Lewis, W. Arthur. *Aspects of Tropical Trade 1883–1965*. Stockholm: Almqvist and Wiksell, 1969.

——. "Economic Development with Unlimited Supplies of Labour." *The Manchester School* 22 (May 1954): 139–91.

Linder, Staffan B. *An Essay on Trade and Transformation*. New York: John Wiley and Sons, 1961.

Little, Ian; Scitovsky, Tibor; and Scott, Maurice. *Industry and Trade in Some Developing Countries: A Comparative Study*. London: Oxford University Press paperback, 1970.

MacDougall, G. D. A. "The Benefits and Costs of Private Investment from Abroad: A Theoretical Approach." *Economic Record* 36 (March 1960): 1–18. Reprinted in *Readings in International Economics*, edited by Richard E. Caves and Harry G. Johnson, pp. 172–94. Homewood, Ill.: Richard D. Irwin, 1968.

——. "British and American Exports: A Study Suggested by the Theory of Comparative Costs. Part I." *Economic Journal* 61 (December 1951): 697–724.

Mansfield, Edwin. *Microeconomics*. New York: W. W. Norton and Co., 1970.

Marris, Robin. "The Modern Corporation and Economic Theory." In *The Corporate Economy, Growth Competition and Innovative Potential*, edited by Robin Marris and Adrian Wood, pp. 271–83. Cambridge: Harvard University Press, 1971.

Mason, R. Hal. "Some Observations on the Choice of Technology by Multinational Firms in Developing Countries." *Review of Economics and Statistics* 55 (August 1973): 349–55.

Miller, Norman C., and Whitman, Marina V. N. "A Mean-Variance Analysis of United States Long-Term Portfolio Foreign Investment." *Quarterly Journal of Economics* 84 (May 1970): 175–96.

"Multinational Firms Face a Growing Power: Multinational Unions." *Wall Street Journal*, 23 April 1973, p. 1.

Mundell, Robert. "International Trade and Factor Mobility." *American Economic Review* 47 (June 1957). Reprinted in *Readings in International Economics,* edited by Richard E. Caves and Harry G. Johnson, pp. 101–14. Homewood, Ill.: Richard D. Irwin, 1968.

Murray, Tracy. "How Helpful is the Generalised System of Preferences to Developing Countries?" *Economic Journal* 83 (June 1973): 449–55.

Myint, Hla. "The 'Classical Theory' of International Trade and the Underdeveloped Countries." *Economic Journal* 68 (June 1958): 317–37. Reprinted in *Readings in International Economics,* edited by Richard E. Caves and Harry G. Johnson, pp. 318–38. Homewood, Ill.: Richard D. Irwin, 1968.

―――. *Southeast Asia's Economy: Development Policies in the 1970's.* New York: Praeger, 1972.

Myrdal, Gunnar. *An International Economy: Problems and Prospects.* New York: Harper & Row, 1956.

Nam, Woo H. "Industry Concentration and Performance: Korean Manufacturing Industries." Seoul: Korea Development Institute Working Paper 7209, June 1972.

Nelson, Richard R.; Schultz, T. Paul; and Slighton, Robert L. *Structural Change in a Developing Economy: Colombia's Problems and Prospects.* Princeton: Princeton University Press, 1971.

Nelson, Richard R., and Winter, Sidney G. "Toward an Evolutionary Theory of Economic Capabilities." *American Economic Review* 63 (May 1973): 440–49.

Ohlin, Bertil. *Interregional and International Trade.* Rev. ed. Cambridge: Harvard University Press, 1967.

Okita, Saburo and Miki, Takeo. "Treatment of Foreign Capital—A Case Study for Japan." In *Capital Movements and Economic Development,* edited by John Adler. New York: St. Martin's Press, 1967.

Paauw, Douglas S., and Fei, John C. H. *The Transition in Open Dualistic Economies.* New Haven: Yale University Press, 1973.

Pack, Howard. "Employment in Kenyan Manufacturing—Some Microeconomic Evidence." Mimeographed. Swarthmore, Pa., 1972.

―――. "The Employment-Output Trade-off in LDC's—A Microeconomic Approach." Yale University, Economic Growth Center Discussion Paper no. 179. New Haven, 1973.

"The Poor Countries Turn from Buy-Less to Sell-More." *Fortune* 81 (April 1970): 90.

Ranis, Gustav. "Industrial Sector Labor Absorption." *Economic Development and Cultural Change* 21 (April 1973): 387–408.

―――. "The Role of the Industrial Sector in Korea's Transition to Economic Maturity." In *Basic Documents and Selected Papers of*

Korea's Third Five-Year Economic Development Plan (1972–1976), edited by Sung Hwan Jo and Seong-Yawng Park. Seoul, 1972.

Reichers, Philip D. "The Electronics Industry of China." In *People's Republic of China: An Economic Assessment*, compiled for United States Congress, Joint Economic Committee. Washington, D.C.: U.S. Government Printing Office, 1972.

Reubens, Edwin. "Foreign Capital and Domestic Development in Japan." In *Economic Growth: Brazil, India, Japan*, edited by Simon Kuznets, Wilbert Moore, and Joseph Spengler, pp. 184–90. Durham, N.C.: Duke University Press, 1955.

Reynolds, Lloyd, and Gregory, Peter. *Wages, Productivity, and Industrialization in Puerto Rico*. Homewood, Ill.: Richard D. Irwin, 1965.

Ricardo, David. *The Principle of Political Economy and Taxation*. New York: E. P. Dutton & Co., 1960.

Rolfe, Sidney, ed. *The Multinational Corporation in the World Economy*. New York: Praeger Publishers, 1969.

Rubin, Seymour J. "The International Firm and the National Jurisdiction." In *The International Corporation*, edited by Charles P. Kindleberger, pp. 179–204. Cambridge: M.I.T. Press, 1970.

Rybczynski, T. M. "Factor Endowment and Relative Commodity Prices." *Economica* 22 (November 1955): 336–41. Reprinted in *Readings in International Economics*, edited by Richard E. Caves and Harry G. Johnson. Homewood, Ill.: Richard D. Irwin, 1968.

Samuelsson, Hans-Frederick. *Foreign Direct Investment in Sweden 1965–70*. Stockholm: Industriens Utrednings-Institut, 1973.

Scherer, F. M. *Industrial Market Structure and Economic Performance*. Chicago: Rand McNally and Co., 1970.

Schreiber, Jordan. *U.S. Corporate Investment in Taiwan*. New York: Dunellen Publishing Co., 1970.

Schumpeter, Joseph A. *The Theory of Economic Development*. Oxford: Oxford University Press paperback, 1961.

Sedjo, Roger. "The Turning Point for the Korean Economy." In *Basic Documents and Selected Papers of Korea's Third Five-Year Economic Development Plan (1972–1976)*, edited by Sung-Hwan Jo and Seong-Yawng Park, pp. 207–21. Seoul, 1972.

Singer, H. W. "The Distribution of Gains Between Investing and Borrowing Countries." *American Economic Review* 40 (May 1950). Reprinted in *Readings in International Economics*, edited by Richard E. Caves and Harry G. Johnson. Homewood, Ill.: Richard D. Irwin, 1968.

Slowinski, Walter A., and Haderlein, Thomas M. "United States Taxation of Foreign Income: The Increasing Role of the Foreign Tax

Credit." In *International Trade, Investment, and Organization*, edited by Wayne R. LaFave and Peter Hay, pp. 137–53. Urbana: University of Illinois Press, 1967.

Solow, R. M. *Growth Theory: An Exposition*. New York: Oxford University Press, 1970.

"South Koreans Investing Abroad in Other Less-Developed Lands." *New York Times*, 19 March 1973, p. 58.

Stobaugh, Robert B. "How Investment Abroad Creates Jobs at Home." *Harvard Business Review* 50 (September–October 1972): 118–26.

Strassman, W. Paul. *Technological Change and Economic Development*. Ithaca, N.Y.: Cornell University Press, 1968.

Streeten, Paul. "Technology Gaps Between Rich and Poor Countries." *Scottish Journal of Political Economy* 19 (November 1972): 213–30.

"Taiwan Sees U.S. Keeping Some Ties." *New York Times*, 21 May 1973, p. 17.

"Textiles." *Oriental Economist*, December 1972, pp. 33–38.

Tsurumi, Yoshihiro. "Japanese Direct Investments in Indonesia." Mimeographed. Harvard Business School, 1973.

Vernon, Raymond. *Sovereignty at Bay: The Multinational Spread of U.S. Enterprises*. New York: Basic Books, 1971.

"Visit by U.S. Aide Concerns Taiwan." *New York Times*, 23 July 1973, p. 7.

Vogel, Ezra. "The Social Base of Japan's Postwar Economic Growth." *United States International Economic Policy in an Interdependent World: Papers Submitted to the Commission on International Trade and Investment Policy*, vol. 2. Washington, D.C.: U.S. Government Printing Office, 1971.

Wells, Louis T., Jr. "Economic Man and Engineering Man: Choice and Technology in a Low-Wage Country." *Public Policy* 21 (Summer 1973): 319–42.

Weisskoff, Richard. "A Multi-Sector Simulation Model of Employment, Growth, and Income Distribution in Puerto Rico: A Reevaluation of 'Successful' Development Strategy." Yale University, Economic Growth Center Discussion Paper no. 174. New Haven, 1973.

Wolf, Bernard M. "Internationalization of U.S. Manufacturing Firms: A Type of Diversification." Ph.D. dissertation, Yale University, 1971.

OFFICIAL PUBLICATIONS

"Alphabetical List of Pioneer and Pioneer-in-Principle Establishments by Major Industry Group as at 31.12.1971." Mimeographed. Singapore, 1972.

Annual Report of the World Bank, 1972. Washington, D.C., 1972.
Annual Report of the World Bank, 1973. Washington, D.C., 1973.
Commission on International Development. *Partners in Development: Report of the Commission on International Development.* New York: Praeger, 1969.
General Agreement on Tariffs and Trade. *International Trade 1970.* Geneva: GATT, 1971.
General Agreement on Tariffs and Trade. *International Trade 1971.* Geneva: GATT, 1972.
International Bank for Reconstruction and Development. *Trends in Developing Countries.* Washington, D.C., 1973.
International Monetary Fund. *Twenty-Second Annual Report on Exchange Restrictions.* Washington, D.C.: International Monetary Fund, 1971.
Korean Trade Promotion Corporation. *Guide for Your Investment in Korea.* Korea.
Republic of China, Council for International Economic Cooperation and Development. *Foreign-Invested Enterprises in Taiwan, Republic of China.* Taipei, 1972.
South Korea, Economic Planning Board, Office of Investment Promotion. "Foreign Direct Investment in Korea." Mimeographed.
United Nations. *Multinational Corporations in World Development.* New York: United Nations, 1973.
United Nations. *Towards a New Trade Policy for Development.* New York: United Nations, 1964.
United States, Agency for International Development. *Gross National Product.* Washington, D.C., 1972.
United States, Agency for International Development. "Total Foreign Equity and Loan Funds Authorized for Projects Approved Under the Foreign Capital Inducement Law (FCIL) Since 1962." Seoul: USAID, 1972.
United States, Commission on International Trade and Investment Policy. *United States International Economic Policy in an Interdependent World: Report to the President Submitted by the Commission on International Trade and Investment Policy.* Washington, D.C.: U.S. Government Printing Office, 1971.
United States, Department of Commerce. *Special Survey of U.S. Multinational Companies, 1970.* Washington, D.C.: U.S. Government Printing Office, 1972.
United States, Department of Commerce. *U.S. Direct Investments Abroad 1966, Part 1: Balance of Payments Data.* Washington, D.C.: U.S. Government Printing Office, 1970.
United States, Joint Economic Committee of Congress. *U.S. Policies Towards Developing Countries.* Washington, D.C.: U.S. Government Printing Office, May 1970.

United States, Office of Education. *Equality of Educational Opportunity*. Washington, D.C.: U.S. Government Printing Office, 1966.
United States, Tariff Commission. *Economic Factors Affecting the Use of 807.00 and 806.30*. Washington, D.C.: U.S. Government Printing Office, 1970.
"The World Bank Atlas: Population, Growth Rate, and GNP Tables." *Finance and Development* 10 (March 1973): 25–27.

Index

165

Economic Growth Center Book Publications

Werner Baer, *Industrialization and Economic Development in Brazil* (1965).

Werner Baer and Isaac Kerstenetzky, eds., *Inflation and Growth in Latin America* (1964).

Bela A. Balassa, *Trade Prospects for Developing Countries* (1964). Out of print.

Thomas B. Birnberg and Stephen A. Resnick, *Colonial Development: An Econometric Study* (1975).

Benjamin I. Cohen, *Multinational Firms and Asian Exports* (1975).

Carlos F. Díaz Alejandro, *Essays on the Economic History of the Argentine Republic* (1970).

Robert Evenson and Yoav Kislev, *Agricultural Research and Productivity* (1975).

John C. H. Fei and Gustav Ranis, *Development of Labor Surplus Economy: Theory and Policy* (1964).

Gerald K. Helleiner, *Peasant Agriculture, Government, and Economic Growth in Nigeria* (1966).

Lawrence R. Klein and Kazushi Ohkawa, eds., *Economic Growth: The Japanese Experience since the Meiji Era* (1968).

A. Lamfalussy, *The United Kingdom and the Six* (1963). Out of print.

*Markos J. Mamalakis and Clark W. Reynolds, *Essays on the Chilean Economy* (1965).

*Donald C. Mead, *Growth and Structural Change in the Egyptian Economy* (1967).

*Richard Moorsteen and Raymond P. Powell, *The Soviet Capital Stock* (1966).

Douglas S. Paauw and John C. H. Fei, *The Transition in Open Dualistic Economies: Theory and Southeast Asian Experience* (1973).

Howard Pack, *Structural Change and Economic Policy in Israel* (1971).

*Frederick L. Pryor, *Public Expenditures in Communist and Capitalist Nations* (1968).

Gustav Ranis, ed., *Government and Economic Development* (1971).

Clark W. Reynolds, *The Mexican Economy: Twentieth-Century Structure and Growth* (1970).

Lloyd G. Reynolds and Peter Gregory, *Wages, Productivity, and Industrialization in Puerto Rico* (1965).

*Donald R. Snodgrass, *Ceylon: An Export Economy in Transition* (1966).

* Information available from the Economic Growth Center, 52 Hillhouse Avenue, New Haven, Connecticut 06520.